ARMSTRONG SIDDELEY

ARMSTRONG SIDDELEY

The Postwar Cars

Robert Penn Bradly

Motor Racing Publications

MOTOR RACING PUBLICATIONS LIMITED
Unit 6, The Pilton Estate, 46 Pitlake, Croydon, CR0 3RY,England

This work is published with the assistance of the Michael Sedgwick Memorial Trust. Founded in memory of the famous motoring researcher and author Michael Sedgwick (1926-1983), the Trust is a registered charity to encourage new research and recording of motoring history. Suggestions for future projects, and donations, should be sent to the Honorary Secretary of the Michael Sedgwick Memorial Trust, c/o the John Montagu Building, Beaulieu, Hampshire, SO4 7ZN, England

ISBN 0 947981 27 6
First published 1989

Write for a free complete catalogue of MRP books to Motor Racing Publications Ltd, Unit 6, The Pilton Estate, 46 Pitlake, Croydon CR0 3RY

Photoset by Tek Art Ltd, West Wickham, Kent

Printed in Great Britain by
The Amadeus Press Limited, Huddersfield, West Yorkshire

Foreword

This book on the postwar cars of Armstrong Siddeley was written to fill a conspicuous gap in motoring literature, for one of England's great marques had hitherto received no detailed study in print. Its production was in response to very many requests for such a book from enthusiasts the world over. Although I had accumulated vast experience in owning, driving and restoring Armstrong Siddeleys, I had no background in writing to draw upon and it was for this reason that for a long time I kept saying 'no' to people who suggested that I might write such a book.

Eventually though, in early 1984, I was persuaded that I would be able to make a worthwhile job of it. The task I then embarked upon has taken over 2,000 hours and necessitated my visiting England as well as many distant places in Australia in search of missing information and rare cars to study and photograph. It has given me great satisfaction and would not have been possible without the enormous help received from my fellow members in the Armstrong Siddeley car clubs of England, Australia and New Zealand. To those many people I offer very sincere thanks for all the help and encouragement. To the many owners who went to great lengths to help me photograph and examine their cars, I also pay special tribute.

I trust you will find this book to your liking, and that it will be a significant help to those dedicated restorers of Armstrong Siddeleys to be found in many parts of the world. May the name of Armstrong Siddeley live on proudly!

Canberra
September 1988

Robert Penn Bradly

Contents

A youthful J.D. Siddeley with one hand on the saddle of a lightweight Humber bicycle in 1892, the year in which he began to work for Humber as a draughtsman, the activity symbolized by the tee-square in his other hand.

1

Prologue

John Davenport Siddeley and the origins of Armstrong Siddeley Motors

by Nick Baldwin, Trustee of the Michael Sedgwick Memorial Trust

Whilst this book primarily concerns the 22,000 or so Armstrong Siddeley cars built after the Second World War, it seems fitting to start with a brief look at the man who founded Armstrong Siddeley and some of the early achievements of his companies.

This brief grounding in no way replaces the need for a detailed history to be written on the prewar years of the famous firm to complement this excellent book by Robert Penn Bradly, a task that Michael Sedgwick was considering undertaking shortly before his death if, as he modestly put it, 'someone more knowledgeable and better connected in Siddeley circles doesn't have a go soon'. By good fortune I have Michael's notes on Armstrong Siddeley in front of me as I write and I was also lucky enough to have had several long discussions with J.D. Siddeley's son, Ernest, shortly before he too died in the mid 1980s.

John Davenport Siddeley was born in Cheadle Hulme, Cheshire in 1866. A small, slim, muscular man with piercing blue eyes, he became a champion bicyclist in his youth and it was his interest in cycling which was to lead him into the motor industry, for many of the pioneering car manufacturers began as makers of bicycles. One such firm was Humber, at Coventry, where Siddeley found employment in 1892 as a draughtsman. He moved to Rover in 1896 and then was employed by the du Cros family which controlled the Dunlop patents and had several investments in both the French and British motor industries. JDS founded his own Clipper Tyre Co and rode a suitably shod bicycle from Land's End to John O'Groats to publicize its products. In 1900 he drove a Parisian Daimler car in the 1,000 Miles Reliability Trial and in 1901 he started importing Peugeots, which he sold under the name of Siddeley from premises facing the Wolseley showrooms in Westminster. Wolseley belonged to Vickers, a vast engineering company which began to produce cars

Lord Kenilworth (formerly John Davenport Siddeley) re-acquainted with one of his earliest cars in a photograph taken around 1958.

to Siddeley's plans at Crayford from 1903. In the following year JDS was put in charge of the London end of Wolseley and in 1905 he replaced Herbert Austin as General Manager at the Wolseley factory in Birmingham. There, many of the vehicles produced were renamed Wolseley-Siddeleys until, in 1909, he moved to the Deasy Motor Company at Parkside, Coventry. Captain Deasy was an Irishman who had started by importing Martini cars and had revived the defunct Iden car factory in Coventry in 1906. Deasy subsequently returned to Ireland and in 1910 JDS became Managing Director and conceived a new range of coffin-nosed 'J D Siddeley type Deasy Motor Carriages' with Aster and Daimler-built Knight engines that were 'as silent as the Sphinx', hence the mascot that adorned them and their successors. The name of the cars was soon simplified to Siddeley-Deasy. In 1912 they were joined by a cheaper brand called Stoneleigh, again based on certain Daimler components.

The Great War was the real turning point for Siddeley's entrepreneurial skills. His factory did subcontract work for many of his Coventry neighbours including Maudslay, Rover and Standard, as well as building large numbers of his own vehicles. Even more important, the Deasy factory was entrusted with the manufacture of RAF 1A and BHP aero engines. These were far from satisfactory and Siddeley's cleverly selected team soon developed the legendary Puma engine, of which 3,255 had been supplied by the end of 1918.

This Wolseley-Siddeley with body by Fountain's Coach & Motor Co Ltd bears the single word 'Siddeley' on its hub nuts.

1909 Wolseley-Siddeley 20/28, chassis number 6020, with four-cylinder 5-litre engine, owned by D.J. Leach who keeps it registered for regular use.

Siddeley had also become an aircraft maker when the Royal Aircraft Factory at Farnborough proved difficult to manage and the strict disciplinarian JDS was put in charge of the staff. Siddeley ultimately built his own aerodrome and factory at Whitley Abbey, outside Coventry, to handle the aircraft work. The Siskin powered by a Jaguar radial engine was an early success and several other famous planes followed as well as the Lynx, Mongoose, Genet, Panther and Cheetah engines, the latter accounting for nearly 40,000 sales. The alliance of car and aircraft manufacturing interests was to be a recurring theme.

Ernest Siddeley, who had joined his father's business in 1913, visited America after the First World War to study motor manufacturing methods and was much impressed with the Marmon,

11

THE WOLSELEY TOOL & MOTOR
CAR CO., LTD.

PROPRIETORS:— VICKERS, SONS & MAXIM, LTD.

TELEPHONE: 6153 CENTRAL (5 LINES) BIRMINGHAM.
TELEGRAMS: "EXACTITUDE", BIRMINGHAM.
CODES: A.B.C. 5TH EDITION & LIEBERS.

LONDON DEPOT,
YORK STREET, WESTMINSTER.
TELEGRAMS: "AUTOVENT", LONDON.
TELEPHONE: 831 VICTORIA (5 LINES).

MANCHESTER DEPOT,
76, DEANSGATE.
TELEGRAMS: "AUTOCAR", MANCHESTER.
TELEPHONE: 6995 CENTRAL (MANCHESTER).

BY APPOINTMENT TO
H.M. QUEEN ALEXANDRA.

WHEN REPLYING PLEASE QUOTE

EH/JFE.

HEAD OFFICE:-

ADDERLEY PARK,

BIRMINGHAM.

March 14th, 1911

Per Registered Post.

Messrs The Deasy Motor Car Co.,
Coventry.

Dear Sirs,

It has been brought to our attention that customers of our Company have been misled into thinking that the cars manufactured by your Company and described as "Siddeley-Deasy" cars, or some other description involving prominently the use of the word "Siddeley" are cars of our make.

We are advised that this clearly constitutes an infringement of our rights acquired by us by reason of our being the registered owners of the trade-mark "Wolseley-Siddeley" and also by reason of the fact that since the acquisition by us of the business of the Siddeley Company in 1903, our Company has acquired the reputation of making cars called and known generally as "Siddeley Cars".

We are advised therefore that we are entitled to restrain you from the use of the word "Siddeley" in any way which would

Siddeley's changes of partner during the early years of his motor industry career were not entirely trouble-free: this is part of an intriguing letter from Wolseley to Deasy about rights to use the Siddeley title. Wolseley soon lost the battle, but the fact that there was a dispute proves that the name already had prestige.

1913 Siddeley-Deasy 18/24, chassis number 5331, with bodywork by S. Paine & Son of Launceston, Tasmania. This elegant and amazingly original example is owned by Andrew McDougal, has never been out of use or required major rebuilding and still feels like a new car to drive. It has done 109,000 miles and been in one family since 1931.

which became the starting point for a new model, the Thirty, which would have been a Siddeley Deasy. Instead it became an Armstrong Siddeley following the acquisition of the company by Sir W.G. Armstrong Whitworth and Co in May 1919 for £419,750. This Newcastle-on-Tyne based engineering company had been producing cars since 1902, originally to designs by Roots & Venables, then Wilson-Pilcher and finally under its own Armstrong-Whitworth identity. W.G. Wilson, originator of the Wilson-Pilcher, was a talented engineer who helped to design the Army's first tank and also developed an epicyclic transmission for cars. This was the

1912 Armstrong-Whitworth type 15/20 series B3, owned by A. Collis, an example of the cars produced by Sir W.G. Armstrong Whitworth and Co before they took over the Siddeley-Deasy concern in 1919 in the merger which brought the names Armstrong and Siddeley together.

13

superb preselective gearbox adopted by Armstrong Siddeley in 1928 and supplied in thousands by the Self Changing Gears company to many other car manufacturers and also for use in racing cars.

In 1919, after the takeover, all the new group's car and aircraft activities were centred at the 25-acre Coventry site under Siddeley's direction. The new cars had a front radiator that sloped to remind purchasers of the coffin-nosed Deasy forebears. This frontal treatment was by *Autocar* staff artist F. Gordon Crosby, who also tidied up the Sphinx at the same time. A healthy total of 2,601 30hp cars were built. This model was joined by an 18hp car in 1921, followed by a new Stoneleigh in 1922, and an American inspired 14 the following year which was a best seller for the company with about 13,500 produced (and 70 still existing in Australia alone). 15 and 20hp versions were added later in the decade. Car output ran at up to a hundred a week and the firm also controlled the A.V. Roe aircraft business (which it had acquired from Crossley), High Duty Alloys, the Burlington Carriage Co (bodybuilders) and Air Service Training.

JDS was increasingly concerned at the profits being sapped from 'his' company by his new masters and in 1926 he raised a bank loan to buy back his business for £1½ million. Notwithstanding the Great Depression, he managed to pay back the money within seven years. Interestingly enough his recent masters Armstrong Whitworth merged with his original employers Vickers in 1927 and his early training ground, Wolseley, was sold to Morris.

Inside the works in the mid 1920s. The characteristic Armstrong Siddeley sloping radiator was designed by the celebrated motoring artist F. Gordon Crosby as an echo of the 'coffin nosed' Siddeley-Deasy, an example of which can be seen in the left background.

For the 1930s Armstrong Siddeley introduced one of the new breed of diminutive six-cylinder cars, the 1.2 (later 1.4) litre 12/6 and was rewarded with sales of almost 12,000 cars. The company also built around 9,500 six-cylinder 15hp cars, over 11,000 18/20hp models, 4,260 17hp cars and 3,750 Twelve Plus/Fourteens in 1936/9. In addition there were a few of the old 30hp type and the splendid new Siddeley Special. Only 253 of these cars of Rolls-Royce standard were made and they embodied everything that the company had learned from its aircraft interests including a magnificent 5-litre hiduminium alloy engine. Some 700 examples of a new 16hp car were made in 1939.

In 1935, nearing the age of seventy, Sir John Siddeley (he had been knighted three years earlier) sold his shares in Armstrong Siddeley to T. Sopwith's Hawker aircraft firm, after first considering selling his interest to Handley Page. Hawker had recently taken over Gloster and was interested in acquiring Bristol until the whisper that Armstrong Siddeley might be available reached them. In the end most of the great aircraft firms entered the same consortium anyway, and worked jointly and with desperate urgency through the years of the Second World War.

Just as the Siddeley name had been to the forefront in the Peugeot, Wolseley, Deasy and Armstrong days, so it kept surfacing through

The Armstrong Siddeley factory buildings in Puma Road, Parkside, Coventry, photographed around 1936.

Sir John Siddeley, CBE, High Sheriff of Warwickshire, portrayed in his Garter Robes in the early 1930s shortly before he became Lord Kenilworth and retired from the company he had created.

all the subsequent changes in ownership, the group title eventually becoming Hawker Siddeley and the car division part of Bristol Siddeley Engines, later owned by Rolls-Royce.

By the end of the 1930s JDS, who had bought Kenilworth Castle for the nation and become Lord Kenilworth in 1937, was enjoying a well-earned retirement. He continued to take a close interest in the industry and had as a close neighbour the Vickers' chairman, Dudley Docker, whose son Sir Bernard was running Daimler, much of the success of whose cars could be attributed to the preselective gearbox that JDS had introduced to this friendly Coventry rival.

Lord Kenilworth died in 1953, having achieved a great deal more in terms of both the breadth and scale of his activities than some much better known names among his motor magnate contemporaries.

Armstrong Siddeley cars, 1919 to 1939

The first model to carry the name Armstrong Siddeley was the six-cylinder 5-litre Thirty, shown here in an artist's sketch from the factory archives, and it remained in production from 1919 to 1931.

The new 30hp Armstrong Siddeley was normally bodied as a formal carriage, but Capt. Denis Shipwright proved that it had the performance to make a racer, lapping the Brooklands circuit in this stripped-down version at over 77mph to win a '100 Long' handicap race in 1921.

16

Above left: Armstrong Siddeley made a brief attempt to produce cheap cars. This Stoneleigh with central steering wheel is competing in the Scottish Light Car Trial in 1922. Above: the Fourteen was a very successful model introduced in 1923. This 1925 example, chassis number 20849, has a tourer body by Melbourne Motor Body and Assembly Co and is owned by Capital 7 Television of Canberra.

The four-cylinder OHV engine, number 15854, of the Fourteen shown above. The car must surely be one of the oldest still earning its place on the books of a large corporation.

The Eighteen was Armstrong Siddeley's mid-range model, introduced with a bi-block six-cylinder OHV engine and two alternative chassis lengths. The Mark 2 version appeared in 1925 with a monoblock engine enlarged to 20hp rating. This 1926 Short Eighteen Mark 2, chassis number 41143, again has a Melbourne-built body and has been in the family of owner S. Whyte since new.

Armstrong Siddeleys were often chosen for State duties: the Duke of York (later King George VI) arrives at an official function, circa 1935, in a very late Twenty. The Eighteen Mark 2 was renamed Twenty in 1928 and became the first model to be offered with the now famous preselective gearbox.

Below: 'As silent as the Sphinx' – an early upright version of the radiator mascot as used in various sizes until about 1932.

Above right: two Twenty saloons, a 1929 version, chassis number 44450 with Ruskin body, owned by C. Cameron, and beside it, with plated radiator, a 1934 model, chassis 46577 with Burlington body, owned by A. McAllister.

A 15hp side-valve engine was introduced in 1927 as an alternative power unit for the Fourteen. The Fifteen subsequently became a model in its own right and stayed in production with detail improvements until 1934. This 1928 series F Fifteen, chassis number 62158, has an Australian saloon body and belongs to Keith Lierse.

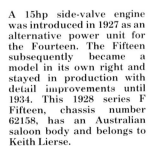

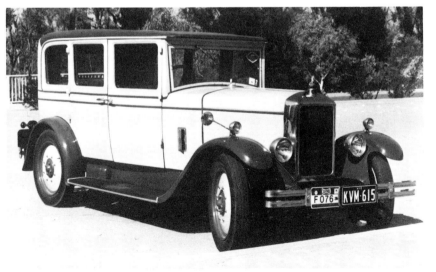

This is the six-cylinder side-valve engine, number MC5635, of the Fifteen in the previous illustration, an altogether more vintage-looking design than the Fourteen, though introduced later, but with the virtue of simplicity in an era of gathering economic uncertainty.

The model which carried Armstrong Siddeley very successfully through the Depression was the Twelve, introduced in 1929, with an economical 12hp side-valve 'small six' engine. The two 1933 examples below are, left, the tourer, chassis 88290, of A. Donkers and, right, a Ruskin-bodied saloon, chassis 89833, one of the earliest cars with an externally-accessible boot, owned by K. Frost.

At the other end of the scale from the Twelve was the Siddeley Special, introduced in 1933. This massive yet graceful machine, designed and built almost regardless of cost, had an advanced specification, including details like hydraulic tappets and servo brakes, and 100mph performance. Only 253 were built, only 24 are known to survive. Seen here is the author's 1935 model, chassis SS3418, with touring limousine bodywork by Burlington. It weighs 50cwt and is thought to be the only remaining example of a handful of long chassis Mark 2 versions.

The 5-litre engine, number 670, of the Siddeley Special shown on the previous page. The design team under Fred Allard drew on the company's experience of light alloys in aircraft engineering to produce this car. Ironically, the high aluminium content is one possible reason why so many failed to survive, victims of the wartime scrap-metal drive.

Below: three-quarter rear view of the Siddeley Special, its elegant lines belying its impressive size. The car was a worthy competitor for the Rolls-Royce Phantom series.

Above right: in 1935 the Twelve was replaced by the Twelve Plus, basically a 14hp engine in the old 12hp chassis. R. Clarke's 1936 model, chassis 100369, has a body by Ruskin of Melbourne.

Another new model in 1935 was the Seventeen, a replacement for the Fifteen. A pleasant, reliable car, it had a six-cylinder OHV engine, an example of which is seen here. 1935 was also the year in which the Armstrong Siddeley company was acquired by Hawker Aircraft.

The 1935 Seventeen 'Four-somes' close-coupled two-door saloon, chassis number 31611, of M. Allen, photographed while undergoing concours preparation – a superb car.

For 1937/38 the Twelve Plus was reworked with a new chassis and revised engine to become the Fourteen. This 1938 saloon, chassis number U1624, is owned by J. Mayhew.

Below: in 1939 the 17hp model was replaced by an all-new Sixteen of advanced design. It was a sweet, nimble car and although the war cut short its career after only a few months some 700 were produced. This example, chassis U3514, belongs to T. Clark.

1939 Sixteen engine, number 26081, as installed in chassis U3514.

Below: typical Armstrong Siddeley chassis of the mid 1930s era. Note the Newton traffic clutch and separate gearbox. Bottom: drawing of stillborn 20hp model, which was to feature independent front suspension and was due for release in late 1939 – no production models were made, and records of the prototypes if any were destroyed in wartime bombing.

2

Postwar renaissance

The 16 and 18hp cars, 1945 to 1954
At the end of World War Two the world's motor industry was virtually static with little new development, most factories, particularly in the UK, having been turned over to the war effort. New cars were virtually unchanged from those of the 1939-1942 era, with the notable exception of Armstrong Siddeley, and Riley following shortly afterwards. Materials were only available in England for manufacturers who were extensively exporting and even then there were major supply problems, making manufacture rather difficult.

The Armstrong Siddeley factory surprised everyone on May 11, 1945 with the introduction of the Hurricane, followed shortly afterwards by the Lancaster. These models were virtually new from front to back, the only immediate prewar item of specification being the reworked version of the 16hp engine which had the nominal cubic capacity of 2 litres.

Unlike any prewar production Armstrong Siddeley car, these models had independent front suspension, by torsion bars, and hydro/mechanical brakes for extra safety. The Hurricane body was a stylish two-door convertible (drophead coupe) of medium size which accommodated four adults in comfort and five if required. It had a reasonable sized boot for the era. The Lancaster which followed the Hurricane was a normal four-door saloon with sunshine roof, accommodating four adults in comfort and five if required. Unfortunately it had a somewhat less commodious boot but featured extensive rear passenger legroom. The chassis in each case was identical. The demand for the new cars was such that the Armstrong Siddeley factory saw fit to have the Lancaster body built by another company (Mulliners Ltd) but continued to produce the Hurricane in its own factory.

In September 1946 the range was enlarged with a fixed-head version of the Hurricane which was named the Typhoon. This body was also made in the Armstrong Siddeley factory alongside the Hurricane, as many of its components were identical.

This three-model range was extensively marketed and

advertisements featured all the cars, or a single model, under the wing of one of the group's aircraft, with the caption 'By Land By Air By Armstrong Siddeley'. The cars were named after the highly successful war-planes produced by the factory, emphasizing the link.

By the beginning of 1947 the factory was well on the way to sustaining a reasonable volume of production (rising to about 2,000 units per year) and sought to appoint new dealers and revive interest among old dealers. The cry and directive from the British Government of the day was 'export or die' so the thrust of British manufacturers, including the Armstrong Siddeley division of

The Sphinx mascot as restyled for the 16/18hp range – very modernistic!

Hawker Siddeley, was towards exporting in most cases the larger proportion of their production. The natural markets were the British Commonwealth countries and, of course, Australia, New Zealand and South Africa were primary targets. Australia, in particular, saw a relatively large number of Armstrong Siddeleys, far in excess of any previous period except perhaps the 1920s when the 14hp had been popular. In Australia the Sydney dealer, Buckle Motors, continued with its appointment which dated back to about 1931, as did the Brisbane dealer, British and Australian Motors, whose appointment had been made in about 1919, with Stokoe's Motors in Melbourne joining about 1935. Dealers such as Southern Motors in Adelaide were new to the job of representing and marketing Armstrong Siddeley cars, a situation experienced by dozens of newly appointed dealers throughout the world.

In May 1949 the range was further extended to include the Station Coupe and slightly later the Utility Coupe, light commercial vehicles both entirely of Armstrong Siddeley manufacture, and they represented a completely new venture for such a prestigious manufacturer. This departure from tradition was seen by many people as a lowering of standards. Interestingly, these vehicles were designated as export models, illustrating the conservative attitude then prevailing in Britain where the factory probably considered it unwise to release these vehicles on the home market in view of the export demand to be satisfied. However, a small number (perhaps 100) remained in the UK. The Station Coupe was for its time an extraordinary vehicle, being halfway between a car and a utility (pick-up). It featured an enlarged cab with two rows of seats and a fairly short load area. The Utility Coupe was a more normal pick-up along the lines of the American Ford and Chevrolet of the day.

The utility version names seem to have been aimed specifically at the Australian market as the word 'station' is the name used for a large or very large farming or grazing property and the term 'utility' seems to be an almost exclusively Australian term for a car-based pick-up truck. Such vehicles had first become available on the Australian market in the 1930s from several American car producers. It did not take long for 'utility' to become shortened to 'ute' in most of Australia, except the state of Queensland where 'tilly' is often used as a shortened version.

With the introduction of the utility models came a revision of the 16hp engine. This was subjected to major development work and enlargement, becoming known as the 18hp engine, with a nominal cubic capacity of 2.3 litres. It gave the range of cars and utilities a very worthwhile lift in performance and a genuine top speed slightly in excess of 80mph.

However, for both market and taxation reasons, the 18hp unit was at first almost entirely exported: from April 1949 all cars received in Australia were fitted with the 18hp engine, while the home market was receiving only 16hp engined vehicles. This curious situation continued for about a year and it was possible to have two cars in the same batch fitted with different sized engines but of otherwise identical specification. The first two digits of the chassis number were either 16 or 18 and this denoted the engine fitted. The same system of numbering was employed for the engine number sequences. For example, a 16hp chassis number is C165219 while an a 18hp chassis number is C1812858. A 16hp engine number is E165270, an 18hp engine number is E189100 or E1812831.

For the 1949 Earls Court motor show there was yet another model produced, an entirely new four-door saloon known as the Whitley. It was named after the factory aerodrome and the Whitley bomber plane, thus continuing the practice of naming the car models after the company's highly successful aircraft. The Whitley was only available with the 18hp engine.

This saloon had semi-razor-edged styling, and while directly competing with the Lancaster (still being bodied outside) it was a very different car, having a more closely coupled body and by the standards of the day a very good boot. It was an immediate success and significantly boosted export sales for the factory. Unfortunately the extensive use of aluminium in the body of the Whitley and the utility models gave quite a lot of trouble in the export market, in countries where the roads were frequently abysmally poor.

It would seem that four car models and two utility models, all employing the one chassis, was too large a range, and in very late 1949 the attractive Typhoon fixed-head two-door coupe was deleted. In retrospect, this seems to have been possibly unwise as it was such a desirable model, but at the time the bulk of the car-buying public wanted conventional four-door saloon motor cars, and the Whitley and Lancaster satisifed that demand. The greatest quantity of the utility models produced in any one year came in 1950, as they had already become firmly established in the export markets, particularly in Australia.

A limousine model had been absent from the range since the end of the war. With more stable and affluent economies in the countries where Armstrong Siddeley cars were sold and, no doubt, some customers in Great Britain for a more formal car at a price well below Rolls-Royce, the Armstrong Siddeley factory produced a long-

Full size wooden mock-up produced as a styling exercise during development of the first postwar 16hp model – thankfully, the design was extensively revised before production.

wheelbase version of the standard chassis to accommodate an in-house produced limousine and landaulette series. These cars, while very successful technically, looked somewhat staid and sold only in small numbers, though the production was probably within the expectations for the period. A more casual lifestyle had emerged since the war and very formal motor cars were not as much in demand as previously.

During the latter part of 1951 the supply of Lancaster bodies was terminated without any real public announcement and only a handful of Lancasters were actually assembled in 1952. However, there was yet another model variant to be introduced, the six-light body style Whitley. The publicity brochure which was printed in February 1952 makes this statement : 'The Lancaster saloon has been replaced by the six-light version of the Whitley. The four-light Whitley is retained in the range.' What the brochure did not say was that there was an extensive reworking of the seat layout and a taller roof which made a vast difference to the passengers' comfort and went close to offering the Lancaster standard of back seat with all the other benefits of the Whitley. This significant modification was also applied to the four-light version of the Whitley and, at the same time, the factory also saw fit to modernize the tail section of the

Factory photograph of a very early series production 16hp Hurricane from 1946. Note square-edge grille slats, rear bumperettes, lack of running boards or stone guards, and no quarter window. Though stylish and clearly of a different era from the prewar cars, the design was conservative and drew heavily on traditional forms.

Hurricane. The last of these bodies had a rear appearance almost identical to the Whitley.

This range of cars continued to be produced well into the middle part of 1953 and for the Whitley into early 1954. Sales of the Whitley and the Hurricane were made well into 1954, in spite of the release of the new Sapphire model in October 1952. The 16/18hp cars were gradually phased out after almost 10 years of production. Nearly 12,500 cars and utilities were built and they brought the name of Armstrong Siddeley to a whole new generation of users and owners. They were sold into markets in many different countries and thus brought a new appreciation of the marque to many corners of the world.

Production history
There were a variety of mechanical changes during the models' run, such changes being a result of the combination of development and experience in service, together with the changing availability of materials, significant technological advances and modifications dictated by marketing considerations. Total production of all 16/18hp versions amounted to 12,470 vehicles.

Like all previous Armstrong Siddeley models, the 16/18hp series was laid down in batches, the standard chassis starting with batch ZG and ending with batch ZX. Whilst changes were to occur during batch runs, the most significant changes were made at batch change-over points. The batches and chassis number sequences are listed in Appendix 5.

The long-wheelbase chassis were run in two batches only and do not appear to have been given batch numbers or names. The long-wheelbase chassis are all five digit numbers to avoid confusion with the six or seven digit numbers for the standard chassis series. It seems strange, in view of the factory's precedent of naming or numbering models and giving them batch code prefixes, to have done neither to the long-wheelbase 18hp limousines and landaulettes.

All standard-length chassis are stamped on the chassis frame with a prefixed 'C' before the chassis number while the long chassis are stamped with an 'L' prefix. This procedure was *not* repeated on the bulkhead data plate, where the prefix 'PS' or 'SM' denotes the gearbox type for subsequent parts supply to owners or agents.

The factory numbers suggest that the last ZX batch standard length chassis was number 1813450. However, it has been proven that although this may have been the intention, reflected in the ordering procedure for the build, parts and components, the last chassis number was in fact 1813300.

The body numbers only vaguely relate to the chassis batch numbering system, as each type of body was also batch-run. At the time of major body or chassis changes each was modified to achieve compatibility. A great many body changes were made quite independently of chassis batch runs and occurred either as required to meet customer or dealer needs, or in response to warranty claims. It is also likely that certain changes, particularly in early cars, were brought about by varying availability of parts or materials. The golden rule for parts ordering is always to ensure all serial numbers and batch numbers are quoted. Body numbers were always prefixed by the model type, the prefixing system being thus: Hurricane **H**, Lancaster **L**, Typhoon **T**, Station Coupe **SC**, Utility Coupe **UC**, Whitley **W**, limousine **L**. (The body number itself served to differentiate the limousine from the Lancaster.)

The chassis frame

The chassis is a complex, somewhat unusual cross-braced frame with a number of special and interesting features including a massive box cross-section at the rear axle. This arrangement provides for a very strong body mounting and incorporates suitable fixings for the rear shock-absorbers. The main frame actually passes below the rear axle in an underslung fashion giving the benefits of both the underslung design concept and the strength and versatility of an overslung chassis. At the front of the chassis there is a very large semi-oval crossmember which accommodates the independent front suspension, the first such suspension system put into production by Armstrong Siddeley. This frame is unusually wide, extending almost to the width of the body and has central in-built mechanical jacks which operate through a trap door in the front floor (utility models excepted).

The suspension and steering

The front suspension consists of a full wishbone independent system and features ball joints rather than king pins. The mass of the car is supported by means of torsion bars (individually adjustable) anchored on special angular cross-brackets at the end of the engine bay area. The screw-threaded torsion bar adjusters are mounted at the rear, sandwiched between the angular cross brackets. The whole front suspension system would appear to be very similar to the Citroen system and may well have been made under licence, but documentation to prove or disprove this point is not available. The rear suspension is a conventional leaf spring type mounted in 'Metalastik' bushes. The number of leaves in the springs and the spring ratings vary from car to utility to limousine and were designed to suit the requirements and mass of the body to be fitted; for some export markets an additional leaf in the rear springs was often added.

The other principal components of the suspension system are the shock absorbers. These consist of four main lever-action Girling units, and as improvements were made by Girling, these were progressively introduced to the chassis. For a long period from chassis 165293 to 1810151 there were auxiliary Armstrong lever-action shock absorbers fitted to the front, firstly for export and later for all deliveries.

The shock absorbers are by far the least satisfactory fitting on these cars. They were too harsh when new and if used on bad roads soon became relatively ineffective and failed to control the very well designed suspension system. This led to considerable damage to the bodies of the cars and utilities in the form of cracks in the turrets and windscreen posts if the vehicles were subjected to harsh road conditions as was certainly the case in the major export markets of

Australia, Africa and New Zealand. If today's technology in shock absorbers had been available then, these body faults would have been less prevalent and a great many more cars would have been saved. Some cars, including the writer's Hurricane (C189066), have now modern tubular gas shock absorbers fitted which results in a remarkable transformation and brings modern standards of ride and handling without altering the classic character of the vehicle.

The steering on the 16/18hp models is an item of great achievement. These cars have the lightest of steering, which, while fairly low in gearing, is very precise, and coupled with the outstanding balance of the car, contributes to quite remarkable handling qualities. The steering unit was a Burman worm-and-nut type until almost two-thirds of the way through the 16hp model run. When the recirculating-ball type steering box became available it was immediately introduced (at chassis 164463), and this made the previously relatively light steering now feather light. Many early cars have had this later steering box subsequently fitted, as it is a significant improvement.

In each case the column is adjustable for rake by slotted column mounting brackets and on all car models the wheel is telescopically adjustable for reach. The hollow centre of the steering shaft accommodates a stator tube and the steering wheel centre features horn button, headlight dip/main beam control and direction indicator control which is self-cancelling. Even the self-cancelling mechanism is readily adjustable for bias, by a movable striker ring. Utility models were not fitted with direction indicators nor had they the adjustable steering wheel.

The brakes
The brakes on models with the standard length chassis are Girling hydro/mechanical type with the front being hydraulic in operation and the rear mechanical. These brakes operate in 12in diameter drums, with two shoes per drum, one leading and one trailing. The curious feature of the brakes is that the mechanical operation comes into effect marginally ahead of the hydraulic operation: to enable the latter to work, the rear brake shoes have to be actually in contact with the drums. This system virtually eliminates the nose-dive tendency found in many cars. The front brakes self adjust and the rear brakes have the normal protruding adjuster on the backplate. For the brakes to work to their maximum efficiency the rear brakes have to be kept adjusted up. It will then prove to be an exceptionally good system with stopping distances from 30mph far better than most cars of the period. The large finned drums dissipate heat very quickly, eliminating the problem of brake fade. The front brakes have only a bottom return spring, together with an unusual mechanism at the end of the leading shoe lining to ensure the brakes do not drag. There is no line valve in the system, which works very well in normal service, but displays a tendency to shake the shoes clear of the drums if the car is used over unmade, stony or outback desert roads. As a result the pedal has to be pumped once or twice, prior to using the brakes, to ensure that the shoes are in contact range with the drums. Many dealers servicing cars from the outback

were forced to fit adjusting cams to the front brakes to overcome this problem. Another minor criticism of the brakes was their tendency to squeal on some types of brake lining.

But overall the system works well, giving minimal problems in service and, if correctly set up and maintained, provides very good braking, adequate in today's 'cut-and-thrust' traffic. This proves the high level of design, bearing in mind the more leisurely requirements of the 1940s and 50s.

The handbrake is of the pistol grip type mounted below the instrument panel and operates the rear mechanical linkage by cable. It is particularly efficient, an important feature as with preselective gearbox cars you rely entirely on the handbrake when parking.

The long-chassis models were fitted with an entirely different braking system manufactured by Lockheed. Interestingly enough these are the only postwar Armstrong Siddeleys fitted with brakes by this manufacturer. This system, unlike that of the standard length vehicles, is fully hydraulic, operating 12in diameter drums, two shoes per drum, with the front brakes being of the two-leading-shoe type and the rear brakes having one leading and one trailing shoe. The handbrake works on the rear wheels only in the customary fashion. These brakes were adjusted through an aperture in the face of the drum which was common Lockheed practice.

The use of a different system had two purposes. Firstly, and almost certainly the main consideration, was the need to arrest the progress of such a heavy car. Secondly, the change may have well been influenced by the desire to reduce road wheel diameters to 16in to achieve lower overall gearing without changing the differential ratios.

The engines
The six-cylinder in-line overhead-valve engine for these vehicles came in two forms: the 2-litre 16hp (actually 15.72hp) and the later 2.3-litre 18hp (actually 18.22hp) wet-sleeved engine. Both have very similar appearance and many common components. Broadly speaking, after the changeover period mentioned earlier, when cars were produced with either engine according to their intended destinations, the 18hp engine superseded the 16hp engine with, for all practical purposes, no increase in weight, giving the vehicles a very significant lift in performance with a top speed of over 80mph: more importantly a 75mph cruising speed was now achievable.

These engines were of the long-stroke concept, both having a stroke of 100mm, the 16hp a 65mm bore and the 18hp a 70mm bore. They were machined to very fine tolerances and carefully balanced, which results in extremely silky and smooth performance. Many examples found their way into boats and other uses where minimum vibration was important. The torque curve is extremely flat, providing a smooth flow of power at all speeds, sufficient to allow a top gear start on any level road with reasonable ease.

The engines were of overhead-valve design with the valves operated from a camshaft set in the block through hydraulic tappets, hollow pushrods, and rockers. Very late in the production run the hydraulic tappets were replaced by solid tappets due to the cessation of supply of the former from Lockheed. This was an unfortunate occurrence but only affected the last 800 chassis produced. The hydraulic tappets are protected by a very fine gauze filter in the supply line, which needs cleaning only very occasionally now that higher quality oils are available, and have proved to be remarkably trouble free in service. The use of inappropriate oils is well known to cause noisy hydraulic tappets and some owners have converted their cars to solid tappets, not realizing the importance of the correct grade and type of engine oil.

The cooling system consists of a belt-driven vane pump fastened to the front of the engine, which circulates the water from the engine's very generous water passageways into the radiator and back to the block. The capacity of coolant is, by today's standards, generous, the contents of the engine, the later type radiator, heaters and hoses amounting to almost 4 gallons! The radiator is a very large brass and copper assembly with a capacious header tank, providing more than sufficient cooling exposure. The 16hp cars had a narrower core and were not initially pressurized. When the 18hp engine became available, the depth of the core was increased and all cars then had pressurized systems operating at 4psi. The radiator is mounted in rubber hangers and has rubber base pads to cushion road jolts.

The cooling system works exceptionally well provided the radiator is not allowed to become clogged internally by rust from the engine or externally by insects, and the cars show no tendency to overheat, even in tropical conditions. The radiators were cooled by a two-bladed fan assembly for the home market and a four-bladed fan was only used for export cars. Operating temperatures are controlled by a large brass thermostat, generally set to open at around 22 to 25 degrees celsius.

These engines are lubricated via a full-flow filter from the sump-located Hoburn Eaton gear-type pump, shaft-driven from the camshaft. The sump and filter capacity at 13 imperial pints is also very large by today's standards, considering the cubic capacity of the engine. The life of these engines was largely dictated by the frequency of oil changes (a 2,000 mile interval was the general recommendation) and filter element replacements (5,000 mile intervals recommended). The filtration was through a felt element which did a reasonable job, but many owners have converted their cars to run on the modern paper filter using a spacer with a 346 Sapphire element. This change in filtration seems to more than double the overall life expectancy, particularly if the motor is used in very dusty conditions. 100,000 to 150,000 miles is fairly normal with the proper servicing of oils and filters, even without the modification, prior to needing a major overhaul. Some engines have now done over 400,000 miles and are still working well.

The other factor in the life of any engine is the ingress of airborne dust, and engines destined for export markets were generally fitted with oil-bath air cleaners which made a significant contribution to engine longevity. The writer has seen cars still with good engines with nearly an inch of congealed mud in the bottom of the air filter bowl. The factory was mindful of this problem and subsequently introduced a filtered inlet and blanked off the inlet on the righthand

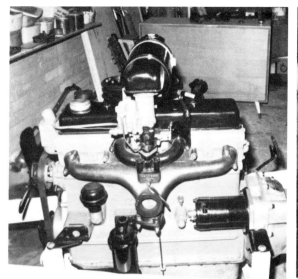

A 1949 18hp export specification engine, number E186407, fitted with synchromesh gearbox, as prepared for display at the 1986 Canberra Motor Show. Note the oil-bath air cleaner, essential equipment in dusty conditions.

side of the engine. It also offered a blanking plate for the drain hole in the bell housing to prevent the scroll on the end of the crankshaft from taking in dust from the clutch area. All of these changes worked well and a great many earlier cars were modified if subject to extremes of dusty operation.

The cylinder heads were very carefully designed to ensure even gas distribution. They have a large balance pipe cast internally into the head and are aspirated by a single-throat Stromberg downdraught carburettor. This is typically a type DAA36 or one of its derivatives, with detail variations depending on engine horsepower, the type of gearbox, the type of air cleaner and the fitment of automatic or manual choke. If the car is fitted with an automatic choke it has its sender thermostat mounted in the outer face of the exhaust manifold, operating by a system of levers and rods up to the carburettor. Generally speaking the automatic choke models are those fitted with synchromesh gearboxes as the preselective gearbox demands full driver control to avoid manoeuvring problems when the engine is cold. Late in the 18hp engine run the automatic choke was deleted firstly on utility models at chassis 189440 and later on all cars, standardizing on the normal DAA36 carburettor.

The exhaust gases were disposed of by a six-port cast iron manifold. The exhaust system is a complex one, having two silencers (except on very early 16hp cars), and is attached to the chassis by beautifully made figure-8 hangers. Each hanger carries two rubber bushes to ensure the exhaust system is fully isolated from the chassis and body, ensuring a very quiet level of operation for the engine. There were three variants of this system, all of which worked well.

The engine has one of two types of carefully balanced flywheel (depending upon the type of gearbox fitted), which is relatively heavy, fully machined and fitted with a shrunk-on ring-gear. In the case of the synchromesh gearbox cars the flywheel incorporates the usual spigot bearing for the gearbox input shaft, no such bearing being required for a preselective box. In the case of the 16hp engine there is a harmonic balancer mounted on the front of the crankshaft: this was deleted on the 18hp unit as its balance is so good.

The camshaft was chain driven, with sprockets located at the front of the engine, the chain being a conventional Reynolds duplex roller type of 60 links. One typically thoughtful touch was the placing of a large brass plug behind the sprocket bulge in the engine block to enable a mechanic to get to the back of the timing chain to fasten or remove the joining link should an endless chain not be used.

It was unfortunate that the contemporary British horsepower tax dictated small capacity engines as the chassis would have comfortably handled a far larger power unit. But the 16hp and 18hp engines were a big step forward in efficiency and have stood the test of time very well. They power a relatively heavy vehicle in an energetic manner: had they been fitted to a car of about two-thirds the weight (more typical for the size of the engine today), it would indeed have been a rapid performer. One or two people have followed the idea up over the years – one of these engines with a preselective gearbox was fitted to a Standard Vanguard taxi in the Albury area of Australia and this vehicle reputedly went very well indeed!

Armstrong Siddeley would never make any mechanical component without a large safety margin, so there was considerable scope for increasing the engine output but most owners who bought a high quality, conservative car were not interested and found the standard performance to be quite adequate. There were however a handful of cars with 'worked over' engines which produced a large increase in power making them quite a surprise at traffic lights, an effect doubtless achieved at the cost of additional petrol, some loss of that silky smoothness, and perhaps shorter life.

As already noted, engines were identified by a six or seven figure number, prefixed 'E', with the two engine sizes distinguished by the first two digits. 16hp engines had six-digit numbers in the series E160001 to E167XXX (the last number is not known). The 18hp numbers had six or seven digits: the precise starting and finishing numbers are not known, but the series ran between E186XXX and E1813XXX. Exceptions to this series were 29 18hp engines with numbers starting at E180001, and these are listed in Appendix 7.

The transmission

Armstrong Siddeley for the first time offered a choice of two gearboxes, the traditional preselective gearbox driven via a dry-plate Newton 8½in clutch, or a conventional synchromesh gearbox with a long central lever, driven via a Borg and Beck 9in single dry-plate clutch. The manual gearbox, as was customary in the era, provided synchromesh selection only on top, third and second. Both gearboxes were made to high standards by Armstrong Siddeley themselves and are very pleasant in operation. Ratios for the two types are listed in Appendix 3.

A conventional open propeller shaft of one of two lengths depending upon gearbox fitted (and two longer versions were also made for the limousines) is employed. It is tubular, partly tapering and with conventional Hardy Spicer universal joints at each end. There is no centre bearing as on the Sapphire models, and the shaft itself is balanced by the use of worm-drive hose clip/s which not only gives fine balancing by the careful positioning of the worm-drive head but helps to deaden noise transference up the long hollow shaft. These drive shafts have proved to be totally trouble free in service, needing only occasional new universal kits after a high mileage has been covered. Fortunately the universal joint kits are of a very popular variety which can still be purchased at almost any major parts outlet

At the front of the propeller shaft there is the usual splined sliding joint which allows for the variation in length required by the up and down movement of the rear wheels. The shaft is coupled to the gearbox and differential by flange couplings each with four bolts with castellated nuts, making removal very simple.

The factory chose to 'buy out' for the rear axle, contrary to prewar practice, and selected the Salisbury brand, model type 2HA. The unit has semi-floating axle shafts and a hypoid bevel drive with a ratio of 5.1:1 (or, expressed as teeth, 51 and 10). This ratio appears rather low by today's standards but must be viewed together with the wheels and tyres which, with a 17in diameter rim and a standard profile tyre, produce a large rolling diameter.

Wheels, tyres and hubcaps

The wheels were of Dunlop manufacture and, as mentioned, those fitted to all but the long-wheelbase cars had a diameter of 17in. They were fairly narrow at 3.25in and were usually equipped with 550x17 cross-ply tyres, while some export market vehicles were released using 600x17 tyres, no doubt in an effort further to cushion the ride and give better traction in countries where the roads were often very poor. The export brochure for the Whitley for sale in Australia, for example, shows the tyre size to be 600x17 with no mention of a 550x17 tyre being available.

The wheels came in three types, all having the standard five-stud fixing. The early disc type had rolled/closed beaded rims very similar to prewar and vintage rims. Identified by part number EN53860, they were unusual in having no ventilation holes or slots. Later disc wheels, part number EN58785, were virtually the same in appearance as the first type except that they had the now conventional open beaded rims.

Wire wheels of the bolt-on type, very similar to many of the prewar Armstrong Siddeley wheels, were offered as an option on both the 16 and 18hp models but were only rarely fitted. Since World War Two there appears to have been an adverse reaction to the cleaning of wire wheels. It is not known how many cars were so fitted but probably only a handful. This option was still offered even as late as the parts list published in July 1951, under part number EN47904. Mostly these wheels were painted in body colour but a few cars were supplied with chrome plated sets. The US market seems to have taken the bulk of cars equipped in this way.

Frequently the rims of the disc wheels were painted black to merge into the colour of the tyre, rather than stand out. The factory supplied specially spun aluminium masking covers to some dealers to enable respraying to be done accurately. The effect of painting the rims black was to make the wheels appear smaller, a very worthwhile move. These wheels also normally had a single fine line painted around the wheel centre, spaced evenly between the periphery of the hubcap and the commencement of the rim. This line usually either matched the paint colour of the feature flash on the car's body, or if the flash was not picked out in a seperate colour, it was painted to match the main upholstery colour. Very late in the 18hp model run, a few cars had three-line ornamentation, with one broad line (about half an inch wide) flanked by two normal fine lines, one on either side. This added a touch of style to the appearance but relatively few cars were so treated, probably because of the problem of finding tradesman skilled enough to ensure accurate concentricity.

There were several types of hubcap used during the life of the 16 and 18hp models. Following prewar practice, they were at first made of brass and heavily chrome plated. Successive styles were as follows:

First issue: These hubcaps featured a large central octagonal 'nut' without any inscription pressed into it – part number EN52775. They were used from chassis 160001 to about chassis 166700 or the equivalent 18hp number.

Second issue: These hubcaps retained a central feature nut, slightly smaller in size, with 'Armstrong Siddeley' pressed into it. The part number for this style is not certain but is probably EN52775A. These hubcaps were used from about chassis 166701 to about 189000 and also appeared on early model Whitleys.

Third issue: This style was relatively similar to the other two, but with the imitation nut deleted, the words 'Armstrong Siddeley' being pressed into the centre. These hubcaps are of a more modern but still classical appearance. They were produced under part number EN59113 and ran from about chassis number 189001 to the end of the production run at 1813300.

Fourth issue: The Station Coupe and Utility Coupe models had a far simpler hubcap of conventional dome shape. This style was used on at least one or two other British cars of the time. It was of the pressed steel variety with the outside chrome plated and the underside painted in a terra cotta colour. It was sold under part number EN58641 and was described in the official parts list as 'Utility Models only'. All the disc wheels were also often fitted with a simple chrome dress ring or 'Rimbellisher', available as an extra only.

There was a totally different hubcap used for wire wheels consisting of a simple smallish dome very similar in style (if not absolutely identical) to several of the late prewar models. This featured an attractive circular Armstrong Siddeley and sphinx badge mounted in the centre. These items were sold under part number EN45678 for the cap and EN36858 for the badge.

The limousines and landaulettes on the long-wheelbase chassis used a 16in pressed steel wheel, fitted with 700x16 tyres. This change was to lower the effective gearing and cope with the greatly increased mass of the car. The hubcaps used on these wheels were of the 'third issue' type. Wire wheels were not offered as an option.

Mechanical modifications

Naturally, over a production run of nearly ten years, there were at least hundreds and possibly thousands of changes to the specification and equipment of the cars. While it is impossible to list every detail modification, the chassis numbers at which significant mechanical alterations took place are tabulated here.

161863 New distributor fitted – Lucas DZ6A.

162201 Rear silencer introduced.

163893 Main shaft in synchromesh gearbox modified.

164463 New type steering box fitted; now Burman recirculating-ball 'F' type, replacing worm-and-nut type.

165293 Radiator pressurized, new brass cap used in lieu of clip type. (Later changed again to valve type pressed steel cap).

165328 Auxiliary front shock absorbers fitted – Armstrong DAS8 type.

165552 Modifications to gears and related parts.

16XXXX*(number not recorded)* Gear selector lever for preselective gearbox cars had control lever moved to left of steering column and choke control knob moved to outside. Early cars had brown plastic quadrant tops which were later changed to cream plastic with radiating guidelines for a few cars and shortly afterwards changed again to an all-ivory plastic cover with bold letters. Very early cars had a short preselective lever with a small round knob, this was later changed to a heavy chromed metal elongated knob and then later again (at about chassis 189000) lightened to a thin chrome lever with an ivory acorn knob on the end.

166191 *(and 18hp series)* New main front shock absorbers fitted – now Girling PV6X, requiring different mounting holes in top of chassis.

167165 Last 16hp car produced.

186001 18hp engine introduced for export only.

187413 *(engine number)* New vacuum-advance distributer fitted – type DVX6A/C50 Lucas.

187413 *(engine number)* New starter motor fitted; solenoid now separately fitted firstly on left-hand rear engine foot and later on body.

188001 Revised and stiffened crankshaft fitted using modified thrust bearings and new main bearing shells.

188001 Exhaust downpipe routed through chassis (now modified) to front silencer, figure-8 hangers deleted from front silencer. Exhaust downpipe now conventional tubular steel in lieu of flexible tube.

188021 New water pump fitted with carbon/rubber non-adjustable seal. Note: a great many earlier cars have retrospectively had this change incorporated.

188449 Modified front brake hoses and fittings introduced.

188848 New centre steering idler introduced.

1810152 Auxiliary front shock absorbers deleted and extra heavy duty main shock absorbers fitted – Girling PV7X type now used - identifiable by large nut-type cap on top in lieu of small filler plug. Many earlier cars are not fitted with this shock absorber.

1811909 New two-silencer exhaust system fitted to all vehicles as standard, with new manifold with angled outlet; pipes routed via the front mudguard, then back into the inside of the chassis through a hole in the chassis rail below the left front door. This modification was also made to the some cars and utilities prior to its universal application at chassis 1811909, these vehicles have the following chassis numbers: 1811404, 1811750, 1811754, 1811757, 1811843, 1811880, 1811886, 1811902, 1811906 and 1811907.

1812105 Modified rear springs fitted.

1812501 Solid tappets introduced, replacing hydraulic tappets, due to non-availability of hydraulic tappets from Lockheed. Note: this change was a retrograde necessity.

1812684 Cross tension spring stabilizer system introduced which eliminated any front mudguard shake. Note: many earlier cars have been subsequently thus fitted when subjected to bad road conditions, giving dramatically improved ride and cornering.

Bodywork

The bodies used on the 16 and 18hp chassis were of seven basic types, and with the exception of the Lancaster all were made by the Armstrong Siddeley factory at Parkside, Coventry, in the premises that had produced the Burlington bodies in the prewar period. This body building facility had, for many years, been part of the Armstrong Siddeley factory. The name Burlington appears to have been considered unnecessary after World War Two. Doubtless the factory was well aware of the bad image that English coachbuilders had in respect of durability in the more demanding export markets: even in the 1980s some enthusiasts in these areas refuse to buy cars

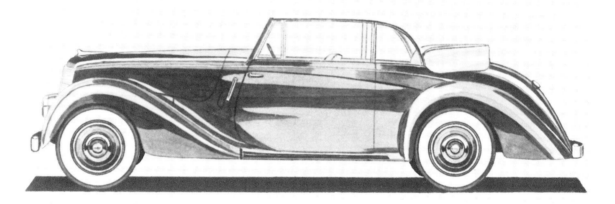

of whatever make with English coachbuilt bodies. Even though they are generally most attractive and frequently sumptuously appointed, their durability is still suspect. The Burlington bodies have certainly a better reputation in this respect than many others.

Owing to the existence of this in-house body building capacity at the Armstrong Siddeley factory only 112 postwar chassis were delivered to coachbuilding firms. Probably the most notable in the 18hp series were the stunningly attractive drophead coupe built on the long chassis by Hooper and the 26 18hp convertibles (very similar to the Hurricane) built by Pennock of The Hague. This practice of building most of the bodies at the factory was a distinct departure from prewar days when a fair percentage of Armstrong Siddeley chassis had been bodied by a variety of coachbuilders both in England and abroad, such as Hooper, Thrupp and Maberly, Salmons, Ruskin, Creswell, and others.

When the 16hp series was launched in May 1945 following the declaration of peace, the announcement carried a description of just two body styles, the Hurricane and the Lancaster. Both were four to

Relatively few 16/18hp models were specially bodied by outside coachbuilders, but notable among them were 26 drophead coupes on the 18hp chassis to this design by Pennock of The Hague. Drawing by John Bull.

five-seater cars and featured a high level of finish, with much polished woodwork and good quality carpet and fittings. Both had a smallish boot with a separate compartment below to carry the spare wheel and heavy tools. The light hand tools were neatly carried in a small attache case located beneath the instrument panel. At the rear, a typical Lucas glass faced number plate box assembly incorporated D-shaped tail and stop light lenses.

The front of the car was a departure from earlier Armstrong Siddeley practice, with a bonnet opening crocodile style and horizontal radiator grille bars with no surrounding mounting shell. The mudguards were very modern for the day and incorporated the headlight bodies welded in; within each headlight there was a small parking light. The bumper bars were of the blade type and very thick by today's standards. Hurricanes and some Typhoons had harmonic balancing weights incorporated in the ends of the front bumper bar. Initially, the cars were fitted with a pair of twin bumperettes at the rear but this style was soon dropped in favour of a bumper bar to match the front. Overriders were standard for export cars but optional for UK market deliveries. Gone was the conventional running board, replaced by a suggestion of one which was, in fact, part of the structural integrity of the lower body, and provided on its inner edge the mounting points for the door pillars. These vestigial running boards tended to get chipped by shoes and about midway through the 16hp run a series of rubber strips were fitted. The front doors were always rear hung; in the case of the Lancaster and Whitley the rear doors were front hung.

Bodywork modifications
The bodywork of these cars underwent many alterations during the production run. Three features that were abondoned quite early were the square edged grille slat, the twin rear bumperettes and the outward ledge on the bottom edge of the instrument panel. In listing all the changes that were made it is seldom possible to quote an exact chassis or body number as the available records are not that specific, but the dates as accurately as can be ascertained are as follows.

Early 1946: Rear bumperettes abandoned in favour of full-width bar.

Early 1946: The first Lancaster production car completed.

Late 1946: The first Typhoon production car completed.

Early 1947: Radiator grille slats changed to quadrant section, but still with two-piece grille arrangement (at about chassis 162500).

Early 1947 Return edge deleted from instrument panel (also at about chassis 162500). This occurred from Typhoon body number T2091 (excepting T2092) but there is no record of changeover numbers for Hurricane and Lancaster.

1947-1948 'West of England' cloth seat trim and (often) door trims used intermittently; sometimes leather used for front seats with cloth to rear seats. This procedure adopted for between 12 to 18 months.

Mid 1947: Front quarter window with fixed glass introduced to Hurricane doors.

Late 1947: Door trims of Lancaster changed to a simpler design.

Early 1948: Side scuttle ventilators introduced to Hurricane, Lancaster and Typhoon.

Mid 1948: Protective rubber strips to vestigial running boards introduced.

Late 1948: Stoneguard rubbers fitted to front of rear mudguards.

Late 1948: Windscreen wiper mechanism totally changed from the hand park type to the switch park type. The sweep of the wiper arms was significantly increased.

Late 1948: Bonnet line lowered to increase visibility.

Early 1949: Typhoon and Hurricane seats widened to maximize use of available space. More pleating added to seats with direction changed from transverse pleats to fore/aft pleats. (Commencing with Hurricane body H4301 and Typhoon body T3450.)

Early 1949: Lancaster front seat changed to bench type. Twin ashtrays in rear armrest deleted and replaced by new style ashtray in back of front seat.

Early 1949: Centre interior light in Lancaster introduced, replacing twin side lights.

Mid 1949: Station and Utility Coupe models introduced.

Mid 1949: Lancaster door hinges changed to allow better access; hinges now partly visible outside door line.

Late 1949: Separate front parking lights fitted below headlights and profile of front mudguard more curved between headlight and grille. This modification was introduced later on both utility models and was standard for all Whitleys and Limousines. The body numbers for introduction are: Lancaster, L8801; Hurricane H4501; Typhoon T3685.

Very late 1949: A completely new instrument panel and instruments introduced to all car models – a most attractive improvement. One piece radiator grille introduced with modified bonnet, now top opening only, leaving the bonnet sides in place at all times. Grille, still equipped with quadrant section slats, not greatly different in overall appearance, but a worthwhile improvement, particularly the vertical side chrome trim pieces. These changes applicable from Hurricane body H4501, Typhoon T3687, Lancaster number not recorded and for all Whitleys, prototype excepted.

Very late 1949: Typhoon deleted from range and Whitley introduced at approximately this time. Note there were only 14 Typhoons built with Whitley style radiator grille, instrument panel etc, being bodies T3687 to T3700.

Very late 1949: Front quarter windows on Lancaster front doors able to be pivoted, increasing the air flow into the car to meet complaints from users in hot climates.

Early 1950: Lancaster front door locks changed to the same type as on the Whitley, together with the abandonment of the pocket-type interior door handle. Trim changed to included capacious door pockets similar to the Whitley style.

Late 1950: Side scuttle ventilators deleted on all bodies except the Lancaster. In lieu, a large central scuttle vent immediatly ahead of the windscreen was introduced. This change might be thought to have accompanied the major change in the scuttle/bulkhead (next item) but this was not quite so: it came at somewhere about chassis 188700, but, like so many modifications, its date of introduction varied from body type to body type. For example, Hurricane 189501 and the writer's Hurricane 189066 both have the late type scuttle vent but the early type bulkhead. Hurricanes, in fact, had the later vent from body number H4593 while they did not receive the later type scuttle until body H4685.

Late 1950: The scuttle/bulkhead was redesigned for all models; the double bull-nose shape was replaced with a simpler, angular bulkhead. This led to a number of other significant alterations: (**a**) the battery was moved to the left-hand side from a central position for easier servicing; (**b**) the heater unit was centralized and placed nearer the feet for greater warmth; (**c**) the lovely tool box that was formerly mounted under the instrument panel, in the space beneath the battery box, was deleted and the same set of tools was now housed in a conventional leatherette tool roll in the boot; (**d**) the accelerator linkage was changed to suit. This new layout resulted in a more accessible engine but marginally less legroom in the cabin. These changes occurred at about chassis number 189000, the precise point of introduction depending upon body type, commencing at Hurricane body H4685, Lancaster body number not recorded, Whitley body W9508 plus bodies W9478, W9494, W9499, W9500, W9501, W9502 and W9503, Station Coupe body SC10839 and Utility Coupe body number UC10613.

Mid 1950: The 'AS' badge above the rear number plate box was deleted on Hurricanes and Lancasters from Hurricane body H4579, Lancaster body number not recorded.

Late 1950: Long-wheelbase limousine 18hp introduced.

From chassis 18964: Whitley windscreen height increased commencing at body W11601. Windscreens on all other models remained unchanged.

Early 1951: Radiator grille badge changed from 'AS' on a red background to 'AS' on a grey background with the figures '18' added. This new badge did not break the line of the grille and improved appearance.

During 1951: The Whitley body went through a number of minor but visible changes: (**a**) rubber boot mat (in lieu of carpet) at body W11531; (**b**) ashtray surround deleted from rear of front seat at body W11750; (**c**) radio apperture in instrument panel from body W12064; (**d**) roof aerial mounting arrangements built in from body W12064; (**e**) rod type boot stay introduced at body W12229; (**f**) front seat cushion suspension changed to coil springs from body W12331.

Very late 1951: A six-light version of the Whitley was introduced, designed to replace the Lancaster. First six-light production body number W14561 (the factory produced one prototype converted from a four-light body).

Mid 1952: Painted radiator grille introduced due to chrome platers strike (this problem affecting other manufacturers as well). Slats painted metallic silver, but many cars had plating subsequently added by dealers or owners as the painted grilles looked a poor substitute. Introduced at the following body numbers; Hurricane H13612, Whitley W13228, Lancaster L12922, Station Coupe SC13071 and Utility Coupe UC12873. There was one exception, Lancaster L12924, which was fitted in production with a chrome plated grille.

Mid 1952: Headlight rims were painted to match car body, probably for the same reason as the preceding change. This procedure commenced at Hurricane H13616, Whitley W13236, Lancaster L12928, Station Coupe SC13078, Utility Coupe UC12880 and Limousine L13148.

Mid 1952: Lancaster deleted from range. Last Lancaster was number L13160, an isolated one-off body.

Mid 1952: Hurricane body changed at rear to match Whitley style. Blade type bumper bars, harmonic balance weights still used but differently mounted. From body H13591.

Mid 1952: Long-wheelbase chassis deleted from range with limousine and landaulette body styles no longer made.

Mid 1952: Station and Utility Coupe models deleted, leaving only Hurricane and Whitley in production

Interior of first series production Hurricane, showing the early hood mechanism and the captive cantrails. On later cars these rails which fitted over the door openings could be removed if required for separate stowage in a bag supplied.

Mid 1952: Whitley turret for four-light body changed along the lines of the six-light turret, and rear seat changed to be the same as the six-light, at body W14251. These turrets are slightly longer and higher at the rear; at first sight they appear identical, but if studied carefully and measured the changes become quite apparent.

Mid 1953: Hurricane production ceased, with some stockpiling of completed cars for sales into the early part of 1954.

Early 1954: Whitley production ceased.

The 346 Sapphire had been introduced in October 1952 with serious production commencing in early 1953. This model overshadowed the two remaining 18hp models and only relatively minimal production of the Hurricane and the Whitley continued past the beginning of 1953.

18hp Hurricane of 1951 showing the hood in the Coupe-de-Ville position. The design was very much intended to be used in this mode, a rare feature by this date.

How many of each?

The total production run of the 16 and 18hp bodies has always remained something of a mystery. The writer asked for this information in about 1962 from the late Danzil Lusher of Armstrong Siddeley Motors and was informed that the data was not kept on a body style by body style basis, as they always worked from chassis numbers and had an individual file on each car to which they could refer if they wanted more details for service or parts supply.

After most of the records became the property of the Armstrong Siddeley Owners Club (ASOC) in the UK, much data became available (excepting the experimental department records) including many of the later individual car files. But alas almost no 16 or 18hp files were handed over. The main source of information that remained was a huge ledger book and batch books, the latter showing parts used to build chassis with the number and source of each individual item, while the former detailed relevant information on completed cars. From these records it is now possible to extract most of the required data. However, not everything was recorded in these master files. It appears that occasionally the finished assembly cards failed to reach the records department, while other bodies were modified for experimental reasons or to customer special order. Thus to say categorically exactly how many of each body type were made is still not possible. In quite a number of instances the record is not

Early-style interior exemplified by the 1946 Hurricane, chassis C161542, of J. Schianoni. Distinctive features are the return lower edge of the dash panel, the aperture for the standard option EKO brand radio, and the white steering wheel rim. The steering wheel boss is green to match the instrument letters.

clear enough to say with absolute certainty what type the finished vehicle actually was. A prime example is the first Station Coupe (the only 16hp one made), shown on the master record against a Lancaster body number together with an unclear description – probably the factory had yet to determine a model name. It is highly likely that the body in question was one damaged in transit from Mulliners, then taken into the experimental department (as tax had already been paid) and made into the pre-production Station Coupe which was sent to Buckle Motors, Sydney, for evaluation purposes. This type of development procedure was not uncommon.

Another view of the same early Hurricane, showing the Lancaster-style door lock, finger grooves in the garnish rail, and early-style trim.

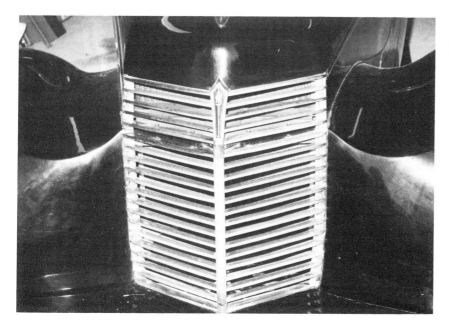

My friend and colleague, Alan Swainson of the ASOC, very painstakingly took an individual count of cars that were entered on the ledger (a record that is the width of about four foolscap sheets and longer, some 500 sheets thick with 30 to 40 entries per sheet) and produced the following figures: Hurricane 2,450; Lancaster 3,472; Typhoon 1,703; Station Coupe 958; Utility Coupe 708; Whitley 2,609; limousine 125; chassis only 112; others 2.

This count shows a shortfall of 331 which further indicates the problem: it is absolutely certain that 12,345 standard-length chassis and 125 long-wheelbase production chassis were built. It was thus

Two views of the 1952 Hurricane, chassis number C1812390, body number H13705, of D. Lomax showing the Whitley-style tail and revised rear seat armrest of the later models. The enlarged rear window is non-original.

necessary to try and establish from the body number sequences, the batch books and physical checks on many cars just how the body production, grouping and batch ordering occurred. In this way it was possible to establish what those sequences were in fact or in some instances what they were likely to have been: the data available gave most of the information but the balance of missing details had to be interpolated and deduced. The conclusions were further exhaustively tested against the history sheets held for these models by three Armstrong Siddeley car clubs, in Australia, England and New Zealand. My revised figures arrived at in this way are recorded in Appendix 6.

Hurricane

The Hurricane, which took its name from the very successful wartime fighter aircraft produced by the parent Hawker Siddeley group, is the body style which had by far the longest production run and was the only model to survive right through the life of the 16/18hp series. It may well be the best known of this range of cars, too, not merely because of its long production life but also because it shared in a certain mystique which attaches to any convertible, or drophead coupe in the language of time. Not to be overlooked is the fact that countless children came to know the car through the very attractive model in the Dinky Toys series.

The 16hp Hurricane was in production from November 16, 1945 (chassis 160001) until August 26, 1949 (chassis 167115), while the 18hp version ran from March 16, 1949 (chassis 186004) to May 7, 1953 (chassis 1813004). The total number believed to have been produced, arrived at through the research already described, is 2,606. The UK and USA were the best markets for the model and have by far the greatest number surviving. Other export territories did less well: Australia received about 45 Hurricanes in all, of which some 17 survive, and no more than a dozen went to New Zealand.

The Hurricane body was a composite structure of steel, sheet aluminium, cast aluminium and timber. It was produced like most modern convertibles in two-door form only and accommodated four adults in comfort or five in fair comfort. The front seating was of

48

semi-bucket style, and during the latter part of the 16hp run these seats were widened to become a type of split bench seat, which enabled a child to be carried in the centre front in an emergency. The rear seat was a conventional bench with a folding centre armrest.

The body was only changed in detail during most of the car's production run, and then only along the lines followed by its companion models. There was one important change, in 1952, when the Whitley-style boot was introduced and the blade-type bumper bars deleted in favour of the more modern but less durable pressed steel bumpers. The last 234 Hurricanes featured this new rear-end treatment.

The Hurricane hood was one of the rarer three-position types and was made to be used mostly in the coupe-de-ville position. No envelope was provided to cover the hood when in the fully down position. In all but very early cars, the cantrails over the doors could be either left attached to the hood mechanism or removed and stowed in a special bag that was provided for the purpose. Unfortunately the hood was not lined. From body number H4501 the mechanism was changed to make its use easier. The factory did not offer a power operated hood as an option although a proprietary manufacturer did offer such a conversion late in the model's run.

The body had very few inherent problems but neglect combined with the normal vulnerability of a convertible certainly caused the demise of many Hurricanes when they fell into unsympathetic hands. It is interesting to note that the whole of the ZG series of cars (the first batch) were Hurricanes, and every one was fitted with a synchromesh gearbox. The first two cars went to the USA (chassis 160001 and 160002, the latter example having recently been rediscovered there) and more than 50% were exported to a great variety of countries, one car, chassis 160035, going to Australia.

Today the Hurricane is considered by the enthusiast to be by far the most collectable and desirable of all 16/18hp Armstrongs and many of the survivors have been or are being faithfully restored. The writer's own Hurricane (C189066) has given very faithful service and since its purchase in 1971 has been in constant use, with many a long trip to its credit. Several times it has been asked to do over 600 miles in a day which it has done without problem and with minimal fatigue to the occupants, while 400-mile day trips have been relatively commonplace. Altogether a delightful motorcar.

Lancaster

The Lancaster was a conventional four-door saloon with a sliding sunshine roof. It was announced with the Hurricane but was not actually available in production form until slightly later. This was the only postwar body that was produced outside the Armstrong Siddeley factory, excepting special order cars. It was manufactured by Mulliners Ltd of Birmingham and was a composite structure of sheet steel, sheet aluminium, laminated wooden frame and other non-laminated wood. As with the Hurricane (and later the Typhoon and Whitley), a wartime plane, this time a famous bomber, provided the name.

The Lancaster 16hp was produced from Febuary 4, 1946 (chassis

161039) until August 26, 1949 (chassis 167144), while the Lancaster 18hp ran from December 6, 1948 (chassis 186159) until February 29, 1952 (chassis 1812205). This was by far the most numerous of any of the 16/18hp series bodies, with 3,597 units believed to have been built, and represented about 28% of all chassis produced. It was the second longest running model.

The Lancaster, unlike the Hurricane, was aimed at the company's traditional, conservative, quality-conscious market and well satisfied the intended customer in war-ravaged England at that time. However, two factors may not have been taken into consideration when the cars were designed. One was the extraordinary thirst for new cars wordwide after World War Two, as neither Europe nor Japan had produced any private cars for six years, and much USA production in the period 1942-1945 was also diverted into war effort.

The other factor was British government policy, based on the belief that exports were fundamental to the country's economic survival, which largely allowed the use of raw materials only for manufacturers whose main sales thrust was export.

This meant that the Lancaster, in particular, as did to some extent the Hurricane and Typhoon, fell into often very unfeeling ownership and harsh operating conditions. For instance, at least 300 Lancasters found their way into Australia and, instead of being used in cities and on highways, a great proportion were sent to work in the worst of outback conditions; often there were minimal roads consisting of inches of powdered dust, peppered with large pot holes and strewn with boulders. Sometimes these cars were even used to round up stock in the paddocks. Unfortunately the timber frame coachwork was no match for such abuse, and the bodies have been known to break at the windscreen posts in defiance. Yet whilst the Lancaster body, with all the wood in its frame, gave problems, the cars were a delight to use and were very attractively finished internally, mostly in leather, with thick pile carpets, polished woodwork and so on. The interior space was generous with quite exceptional legroom for both front and rear passengers. Initially, Lancasters had bucket front seats, but in late 1948, just prior to the introduction of the 18hp series, the bench front seat became available to satisfy customer demand.

The boot was perhaps the only real drawback, as it was not all that large and featured a bottom hinged lid. This did, however, enable bulky items to be transported, but not covered, if the lid were left open. Some Lancasters had a type of rear tonneau cover which rolled up above the petrol tank and would extend to cover a load when the lid was in the open position. The factory also offered fitted suitcases as an option: these made a great difference to the effective use of boot space but due to import restrictions in many countries very few suitcase sets were exported with the cars. As on the Hurricane, the spare wheel was housed beneath the boot in its own compartment. This arrangement remained unchanged during the Lancaster's production run.

It would seem likely from the data available that a disproportionate number of cars fitted with the Lancaster body (of

the order of 60%) had the 16hp chassis, as once the Whitley was introduced in late 1949 (for sale in 1950 and onwards), the Lancaster came to be regarded by many as 'the old model' and most export dealers turned their attention to the new model. Thus 1950, 1951 and 1952 Lancasters are comparatively rare throughout the world.

The Lancasters have not survived nearly as well as other models, no doubt due to the circumstances surrounding their sales in the early postwar period. The shortcomings of coachbuilt bodies caused many to be scrapped after a five to ten year period. However, those that do survive are very pretty and collectable cars, particularly the later models fitted with the late style radiator grille and instrument panel. Ironically, on much better roads today these bodies can now be regarded as at least satisfactory.

Typhoon

The Typhoon was added to the range in September 1946 and was produced in the Armstrong Siddeley body factory alongside the Hurricane. It is for all practical purposes a fixed-head Hurricane, the roof being the only difference, and it provided a low-cost stopgap

This 1950 Lancaster, the chassis number of which will lie between C187700 and about C188000, illustrates the first arrangement of running board rubbers and rear wing stone guards, separate parking lights below the headlamps, and intermediate style hub caps.

Brochure photographs of the 1946/7 Lancaster interior. In addition to the dash, this view shows the early elliptical shaped pedal heads and the flamboyant door trim style, both discontinued in late 1947.

The instrument cluster panel was removable for easy access, as shown here, on all 16hp and first series 18hp cars.

Interior trim and rear seat arrangement of the early Lancaster. Polished woodwork and leather upholstery contribute to an air of traditional luxury.

between the Hurricane, which was already very successful, and the Lancaster until the advent of the factory produced four-door Whitley saloon. The Typhoon, in fact, increased the market for chassis/body assemblies at virtually no extra tooling cost. In the process, the resultant car was one of the most attractive of the range.

Production data (excluding test cars and protoypes) is as follows: Typhoon 16hp produced from August 13, 1946 (chassis 161751) until August 26, 1949 (chassis 167107); Typhoon 18hp from February 18,1949 (chassis 186000) until November 25, 1949 (chassis 187398). The number produced was 1,701, as accurately as can be ascertained. It can be seen that, for a production run of only slightly over three years, the Typhoon was very well accepted and no doubt it helped the company's profits considerably.

The roof was a composite structure consisting of a wooden frame over which a pressed perforated steel sheet was fixed, thus making the foundation. This was first lightly padded and then covered with leathercloth in a similar fashion to the contemporary Riley. Inside, it was lined in the same ivory-coloured material as the Lancaster. The roof, like the hood on the Hurricane, required careful attention

This is the late series dash and instrument panel design, applied to all Hurricanes, Typhoons, Lancasters and Whitleys from the latter part of 1949 to the end of production.

and rewarded a conscientious owner by looking stunningly attractive. The Typhoon with its composite body weighed slightly less than the Lancaster, at 29.4cwt, which helped the car's performance a little.

The factory marketed the Typhoon as a 'Sports Saloon', such a term applying to appearance rather than implying any mechanical change. Nevertheless, it was a car which went reasonably well and was extremely silky, quiet and pleasant to drive. Its appointments, fittings and equipment were almost identical to its sister the Hurricane on a series for series basis. There were but 14 Typhoons produced with the Whitley-style grille, bonnet, instrument panel and so on, making this sub-batch the most collectable.

The 18hp Typhoon is a very rare car in England as almost all home deliveries were 16hp cars due to the horsepower tax then prevailing. Typhoons have survived in almost the same proportion as Hurricanes in Australia, where their importation level was similar. There seem to have been a significant number exported to the USA and Canada where quite a few are preserved. Those that do survive

Superbly preserved Typhoon, a rare 18hp model from 1949, chassis number C187047, is the property of Mrs P. Elliott.

Side view of 1948 Typhoon, chassis C165516, owner W. Read, emphasizes that the model was really a Hurricane transformed by the addition of a fixed roof. The factory called it a 'Sports Saloon'.

are well worth restoration and preservation as the model was surely quite a gem in the Armstrong range.

Utility models

The two utility models were an entirely new and rather unlikely departure for Armstrong Siddeley, hitherto producers of high quality luxury motor cars. These strange vehicles began to be exported to Australia during the wool boom and vehicle shortage of the very late 1940s and early 1950s. Representatives of both Stokoe Motors of Melbourne and Buckle Motors of Sydney claimed that the models were manufactured at their request or suggestion. It would seem highly probable that these two prime Australian dealers were the catalyst or perhaps even underwrote a certain production level. While I cannot prove this view, the production and import statistics seem to authenticate it, at least in part, as Australia received about 60% of all utilities built. Other potential markets were much less well supplied. For instance Rhodesia (now Zimbabwe) received only 52, Fiji 12 and New Zealand but a handful.

Only one 16hp was built, chassis number 166124, which was first used in Australia, where it was sent for evaluation, on April 27, 1949. This may well be considered as a prototype. Production data (excluding test cars and prototypes) is as follows: Station Coupe built from May 25, 1949 (chassis 186815) until July 25, 1952 (chassis 1812710); Utility Coupe from August 11, 1949 (chassis 186954) until

The two utility models constituted a rather unlikely venture into a new market area for Armstrong Siddeley. Above is the Station Coupe version, with a long cab providing accommodation for up to six people in two rows of seats and a relatively modest load area behind. The Utility Coupe, left, was a more conventional pick-up, though more stylish than many, with a single bench seat in the cab and a longer load area, in this case covered by the optional canvas canopy. 18hp mechanical components were used for all but the first prototype.

June 17, 1952 (chassis 1812189). Of the total likely production of 1,739 vehicles, the Station Coupe accounted for 1,022 (approx 59%) and the Utility Coupe 717 (approx 41%).

The Station Coupe version was a long-cabin utility that would seat four to six people as there were two rows of seats, with wide single doors on each side providing access for both front and back seats. The front seat was a fairly normal bench type whereas the rear seat was more spartan and intended only for short journeys. This cabin arrangement was considered quite extraordinary at the time as no other manufacturer produced such a vehicle; the basic idea has been revived subsequently in designs like the VW double-cab pick-up and the Japanese 'King Cabs'.

Inside the cab of a 1949 Station Coupe, showing access to the rear seat. Note early style bonnet, side bulkhead vent and the low position of the petrol filler. Interior trim was more spartan than that of the comparable saloons.

The load area to the rear was of relatively modest dimensions with a gross width of 56in and an overall length of 52in. At the rear was a conventional tailgate. The load area was covered with a canvas tonneau supported on a three-legged frame that mounted on the body side and could be removed for high loads. This arrangement ensured that the weather could be adequately kept out.

The Utility Coupe was a more conventional pick-up model, the cab having a single bench seat, with a larger load area, 56in in width and 63.5in in length. Otherwise the body followed exactly the same concept as its sister, the Station Coupe, both models being identically equipped.

The utilities shared basically the same specification as the contemporary cars and followed series for series, the only exception being heavier rear springs for the Station Coupe, heavier still for the Utility Coupe. All utilities were fitted with synchromesh gearboxes as standard, while preselective gearboxes could be ordered as an option. There were a few preselective utilities sold in Brisbane and Adelaide, but I doubt if more than a dozen arrived in Australia so equipped.

The factory listed the following extras as being available on both utility models: rear bumper bar; under engine sump guard (popular on many outback utes); canopy (available with drop side curtains); no-draught front ventilator windows; heater (the factory called them 'air conditioners'); preselective gearbox; central hinged front seat.

The utility models were far more simply fitted out in the cabin than the cars. The door trims were flat imitation leather, as was the back seat in the Station Coupe. The main or front seat was in tough leather, but on a different frame to the Whitley. Under the front seat stowage was provided for the tools which included a mechanical jack in lieu of the built-in ones on the cars, a strap-up tool bag, tyre pump,

1949 Utility Coupe, chassis C187341, owner K. Gobell; one of the first batch produced, with early grille. Non-standard winkers and bonnet side motifs, otherwise very original.

Above: comparison of the two versions reveals the differing proportions of cab and load area. Left, 1952 Utility Coupe, C1811192, with owner M. Laidlay; right, 1952 Station Coupe, C1811751, the last one sold by Buckle Motors of Sydney, in a dark blue and fawn colour scheme more often seen on late Whitleys.

Rear view of the 1950 Station Coupe, C188731, of K. Nagy, fitted with the optional rear bumper offered by the factory, and later winkers and reflectors to meet legal requirements.

and so on. The only carpet was over the gearbox hump and transmission tunnel, with the balance of the floor area covered in coarsely ribbed rubber. The instrument panel came in two types, both metal pressings. The early utilities had a large open glove box, with the instruments and switches in front of the driver on a panel painted in silver hammertone finish. No clock was provided. The later utilities (from body SC10945) had centralized instruments with two smaller open glove boxes each side; and this panel was sprayed with a gold tone of paint. There was no polished woodwork whatsoever, and the doors were capped with an aluminium extrusion which was painted to match the instrument panel. The headlining was in the usual cream material. The utilities were not fitted with trafficators or winkers, nor did they have the normal adjustable steering wheel, and the hubcaps and bumper bars were more modest than those of the car models.

This reduced level of finish meant that the utilities could be sold for about two-thirds the price of the cars: however, they were still half as much again as the Australian produced Holden utility.

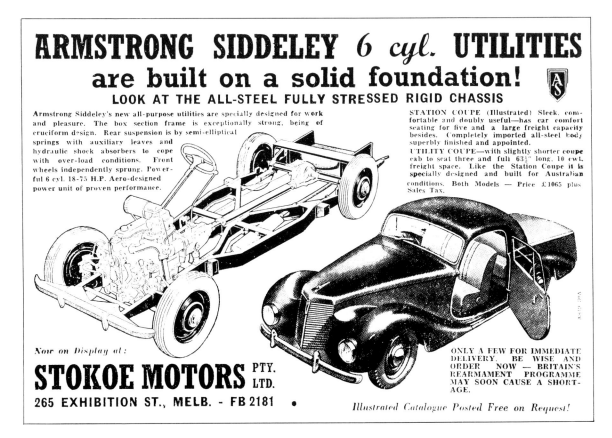

Stokoe Motors of Melbourne were one of the Australian dealers for whom the utility models were primarily produced, and this is how they marketed them in 1950. The emphasis on ruggedness reflects the tough life the vehicles were likely to face in the outback. Stokoe Motors have continued to supply Armstrong Siddeley spares right up to the present.

Fortunately there are quite a number of utilities being restored or undergoing major renovation in Australia at the time of writing, so this part of Armstrong Siddeley history will be well represented. The utility models were very successful in Australia and did staunch work in spite of the shocking conditions at the time. There are still a number on the roads today, some with enormous mileages to their credit, while others are to be found off the public highway, unregistered, but still in use for putting out the feed or doing a bit of fencing around Australia's rural properties. There are other known examples in the USA, Chile, Venezuela, New Zealand, and elsewhere, which indicates that they were quite widely exported. The factory sales records clearly show that they were intended for the export market and the fact that only one or two are known in the UK would seem to indicate that their aim was achieved.

Whitley

This body style was the first saloon to be produced in the Armstrong Siddeley factory after World War Two and it was introduced alongside the Mulliner-bodied Lancaster. It came originally only in four-light form, but in 1952 a six-light version also became available. Though a four-door saloon, it was very different from the Lancaster; the body was more closely coupled but still a comfortable four to six-seater. The treatment at the rear was entirely different, with a large single boot lid. Excluding prototypes and test cars, the Whitley was in production from February 13, 1950 (chassis 187899) until March 16, 1954 (chassis 1813300): the number believed produced is 2,582 (2,303 four-light and 279 six-light).

The Whitley body followed the path of the Hurricane, Typhoon and

For later utility models the instruments were moved to the centre of the dash with open cubby holes each side. This example is chassis number C1811351, owner R. Harvey.

59

Distinctive shape of the 1949 'Tempest': this is chassis number C186547, body number T9003, probably the only surviving example of this Whitley development model. First registered on August 18, 1949, it is owned by Mrs J. Bentley. The winkers are of course a later addition.

The bulkhead and engine compartment of the 'Tempest'. The heater installation is quite unlike any other model, evidence of the car's experimental nature.

utility models in that its construction was a composite of sheet steel, sheet aluminium, cast aluminium and timber. Fortunately there was very little timber in the Whitley, positioned mainly in the turret area. Unlike the Lancaster, the wheelarches were box-section steel in part with the front portion being an aluminium casting. This casting continued up to the turret line, and the windscreen posts were also aluminium castings, while the centre door posts were T-section steel. The body was of fairly light construction and lasted quite well, with the exception of the inevitable cracks that occurred in the corners of the turret when the cars were used on poor roads.

During the latter part of the model's run, when it was decided to

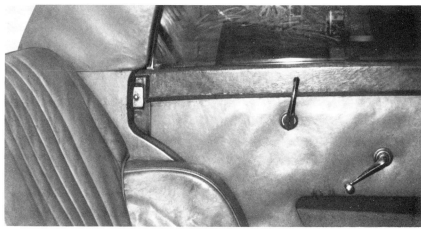

Interior appointments of the 'Tempest', very much in the same manner as the other models, with polished wooden cappings and leather seats, though the door trim panels are less elaborate than some earlier designs.

discontinue the Lancaster, the factory altered the turret, seats and legroom arrangements, to provide a rear seat more in keeping with what the Lancaster had offered. At the same time they introduced the body in six-light form. An Armstrong Siddeley brochure dated February 27, 1952 announced: 'The Lancaster saloon has been replaced by a six-light version of the Whitley...the four-light Whitley is retained in the range...The quarter light has been added to give extra visibility and the rearrangement of the back of the car has increased leg room.'

One late-series feature was the moving of the petrol filler cap to the rear mudguard and changing it to the 346 style, which helped increase usable boot space. This feature is perhaps the easiest, quick way of identifying the late series cars with all the changes. Unlike the Hurricane, Lancaster, Typhoon and Utility Models, the Whitley used the same instrument panel for the whole of its production life,

Though both were four-door saloons, the factory-built Whitley was distinctly different from the Mulliner-bodied Lancaster, with a more close-coupled cabin and a longer boot. Above is the 1951 Whitley, chassis C1810034, of R. Nicholson, and right, the superbly preserved and original unrestored 1950 model, chassis C189170, of C. McCarron.

the Whitley-style panel becoming standard issue for all later Hurricanes and Lancasters as well as being used in the last 14 Typhoons.

The single most important development with the Whitley was the major change to the boot arrangements. The chassis was slightly altered by the deletion of the wheel tray at the rear, and the petrol tank was placed beneath the now slightly higher spare wheel storage area. The spare wheel was now carried in a compartment of its own within the main boot area, so it was still possible to change a wheel without having to remove the luggage. Above the wheel storage compartment there was a large flat boot floor which, on first appearance, appeared to provide only average space: however, the shape was good and the area for luggage proved to be practical and sufficiently commodious. Beneath the spare wheel at the back of the body was a trough which housed a roll of good quality tools, tyre pump, crank handle, wheel brace, etc, all items being clipped or strapped in place, and there was still considerable space in the trough for stowage of all manner of oddments.

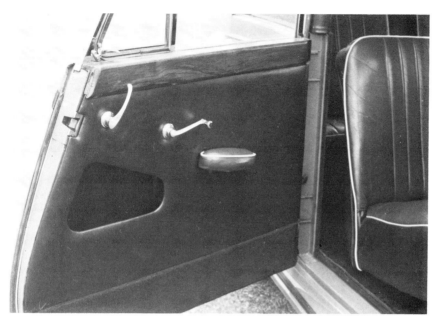

Fittings, trim and upholstery of the standard Whitley interior, exemplified here by the 1951 model also shown on the previous page. As on the Lancaster, the hinges were grouped on the centre pillar so that the front doors were front-opening, the rear doors rear-opening.

The other obvious change for the Whitley was the abandonment of the blade-type bumper bars in favour of an angular steel pressing. This looked far more modern but like so many 'improvements' dictated by fashion or taste the new bumpers were far harder to repair and more vulnerable in the event of a mishap.

The Whitley had a very distinguished and individual style of its own and these changes removed any hint of prewar coachwork concepts. Its overall design has won a place in many a connoisseur's heart and as a result the survival rate for the Whitley is quite high, ensuring it a place in the Armstrong Siddeley heritage.

A Whitley was the last 16/18hp model delivered, at chassis

The Whitley first appeared in four-light form, but in 1952 a six-light version became available as well, replacing the Lancaster. This factory photograph dates from that year. Concurrently, changes to the turret shape and seats improved the accommodation in the rear of the car.

1813300. The balance of the projected ZX series was never produced as, once the 346 Sapphire came on the market, most buyers chose the very luxurious and opulent new car in lieu of what was in 1953 or 1954 a fairly dated Whitley.

Limousine

In September 1950 the factory announced the last body style in the 16/18hp series, the seventh variant, the formal limousine. Not only was it a new body almost entirely but it was mounted on a stretched chassis with a wheelbase of 10ft 2in, an increase of 7in. 125 of these

Close-up of a 1953 six-light Whitley (photographed in the snow!) shows the fixed quarter-light pane and also the differently angled rear seat squab of the last series.

long chassis were produced between November 18, 1950 and June 24, 1952: two were bodied as landaulettes by the factory, one carried a special drophead coupe body by Hooper, and the remaining 122 were standard limousines. This body, which borrowed only its radiator grille, mudguards and bumpers from the other models, was of generous dimensions and provided accommodation for up to eight people, assuming the occasional seats were used. The interior appointments were sumptuous with the usual leather front seat and West of England cloth or leather to the rear in the typical style of the traditional limousine. The car featured a new, more elaborate instrument panel, much polished woodwork, a sliding glass division, an additional clock, and so on, all designed to make the rear occupants as comfortable and insulated from the real world as possible. They were treated to the benefits of a complex heating system but no heater was provided for the driver/chauffeur.

The instrument panel, similar in style but not identical to that of the Whitley, had three separate gauges rather than the cluster and a large speedometer. These instruments were of the same series as those fitted to the early Hurricane and Lancaster. All the switches were carried at the end of the panel near the door. As explained earlier, the long-chassis cars were fitted with 16in wheels and wider tyres – the spare was mounted vertically in the boot, unlike any other postwar model – and had a fully hydraulic braking system to arrest their progress as they scaled some 35cwt in standard form.

The standard limousines were mostly employed for formal occasions and by far the largest user/owner was the well known London car hire firm of Godfrey Davis, who had well over a third of the production. Perusal of the records shows that there were 121 long chassis with preselective gearboxes, one chassis with a synchromesh gearbox and three chassis where the gearbox type was not recorded.

The factory built only one prototype in the experimental

This is an example, from Hurricane C189066, of the tool kit for under-dash mounting supplied with all 16hp cars and earlier 18hp cars until the change of bulkhead in 1950. The later style kit which then replaced it was to continue in use through to the 234/6 series.

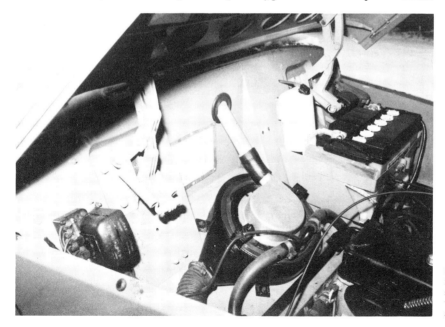

Standard heater installation in an 18hp car with the later style bulkhead. (The screen washer bottle is a modern addition.)

Factory photographs of the 1951/2 long-wheelbase 18hp limousine in standard form. An imposing formal carriage, it was elegant enough in style not to look ponderous in spite of its considerable bulk.

department, chassis number PSEX18L (like other non-sequential prototypes this car has not been taken into the production count). This chassis number code indicates preselective-experimental-18hp-long wheelbase. Its fate is unknown but it was probably broken up by the factory after extensive testing in accordance with the normal policy of not selling to the public cars that were experimental and could not be backed up with service or spares.

Of the three long chassis not bodied as limousines, the Hooper convertible (chassis L18038), delivered on February 9, 1951, has, at the time of writing, just been rescued by Thomas Clark of Newent, England, a well known Armstrong Siddeley enthusiast and restorer. The first landaulette produced (chassis L18084) was delivered on August 3, 1951 to the Sultan of Zanzibar and was painted bright red: its whereabouts are unknown, but it is thought that it may have come back to England about 1957 – let's hope it will turn up again. The other landaulette (chassis L18102) was produced for the

Rear view of 1951 limousine, chassis number L18070, owned by B. Mick.

Factory photograph of the landaulette made to the special order of the Sultan of Zanzibar on long-wheelbase chassis L18084. Finished in crimson with a tan interior, it was delivered on August 3, 1951. Though it was perhaps the most famous of all 16 18hp Armstrong Siddeleys, its present whereabouts remain unknown.

Governor of Aden and was delivered on October 1, 1951, painted black. This car is currently in the Mosely Armstrong Siddeley collection in England.

A number of fine limousines are kept today by ASOC members. This car is certainly a very rare and unusual Armstrong Siddeley and one which will always cause comment and interest whenever shown.

Colour schemes

It may be of interest to enthusiasts to make some comments about the colour schemes that were available for general issue on these models, always remembering that it was possible to order a car to your own colour choice. The common paintwork colours are: Grey (a bluish mid-range grey); Langham Grey (a greenish mid-range grey); Black; Gazelle Fawn (a mid-range fawn with a reddish tinge); Dark Blue (not quite navy blue); and Lakeside Green (strong mid-green, used only on utilities). Rarer colours are: Ivory (mostly only used on late Whitleys and on the flash of utilities painted in Lakeside

67

Three views of the interior of an 18hp limousine, chassis L18070, showing the trim and detail appointments typical of a standard issue version of the model without modifications to special customer order. Like almost all the limousines, this example has the preselective gearbox.

Green); Turquoise Blue (almost a powder blue); Green (an apple green); Maroon (a very rare colour for the main bodywork, used mainly on flashes and on early Typhoons); Dark Green (a very rare colour for the main bodywork, used mainly on flashes); and Silver Grey (pale blueish grey, used mainly on late Whitleys).

For leatherwork, the following choices were available: Maroon; London Tan (brown); Champagne (fawn); Dark Green; and Navy Blue. In all cases carpets matched leatherwork. Some cars were trimmed or part trimmed in West of England cloth. It was normally fawn in colour with self or coloured leather piping.

The general colour schemes were carefully co-ordinated; mostly the interior trim dictated the treatment of the car's decorative body flash. If the flash were picked out in a contrasting colour, that colour would, in almost all cases, match the interior leatherwork. If the flash were in the main body colour, it would be finelined

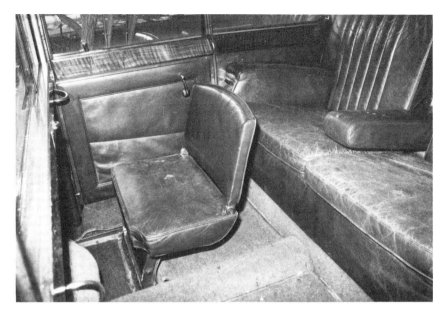

Inside the roomy rear compartment of the 18hp limousine, showing the leather upholstery, well worn but still sound after getting on for forty years of use, and one of the folding occasional seats available to increase the carrying capacity. London car hirers Godfrey Davis took well over a third of the total production of this model for their fleet.

(coachlining) to match the leatherwork.

The seats were often highlighted with contrasting leather piping (mostly ivory) which added a great deal to the interior appearance. Where the car had a flash matching the leatherwork, the finelining on the flash was in a contrasting colour and generally matched the seat piping.

Wheel centres were often picked out to match a car's flash rather than the main body colour, while frequently the actual wheel rim was painted in black to merge into the black of the tyre wall, a treatment, in my view, particularly appropriate to the open-beaded rim type.

Towards the end of the 18hp series the factory offered a number of

69

Most remarkable of all the long-wheelbase cars was this 18hp drophead coupe built by Hoopers (body number 9856) on chassis L18038 to the order of Mr M. C. Rodd of Walls Ice Cream and delivered on February 9, 1951. Above, the car when new, on test before returning to Hoopers for finishing, and right and below as it was when rescued from dereliction by its current owner, Thomas Clark.

two-tone colour schemes which did attract some less conservative buyers. For instance, there is an original Whitley in Sydney (chassis number 1811215) which was painted in ivory for the main part of the body, with black turret, flash and wheel rims, and its leatherwork in green with ivory piping. This colour scheme looks most unusual and very attractive and the car is one that Buckle Motors chose for a demonstrator, no doubt because of its appearance, and was the subject of a *Sydney Morning Herald* road test in 1952. This example is one of several such cars that reached Australia towards the end of the 18hp production run and illustrates the use of standard colours combined to striking advantage.

On the road

Over the last 30 years the writer has owned every style of the 16 and 18hp cars, unfortunately excepting the limousine. In these cars I have driven at least 300,000 miles and to do so have undertaken the bulk of the routine maintenance, as well as upgrading and restoring both a Lancaster and a Hurricane. I hope a few words about their road behaviour and long-distance travel ability will adequately put them in perspective. In my experience, they are extremely docile yet nimble enough in modern city traffic. On the open highway they can easily cover 65 miles in an hour, even in undulating country on only moderately satisfactory secondary roads. They exhibit wonderful engine torque and top gear performance which, coupled with their good roadholding and handling, ensure that long distance travel is relatively effortless.

Many owners, including the writer, have found that 600 miles is a very full but realizable day's travel. Two Australian club members drove 749 miles on Good Friday night to reach Swan Hill by daybreak for an Armstrong Siddeley rally in Whitley 189170. One owner did almost 7,000 miles in a fortnight in outback Australia over mostly unsealed roads towing a caravan with his Station Coupe chassis C188121. The data tabulated by contemporary road testers did not tell of the real staying power of the cars. Mechanically, their life expectancy is very long: a quarter of a million miles before a rebuild is not uncommon, and figures like 100,000 miles before a top overhaul and preselective gearboxes untouched at 300,000 miles all tell part of the story. The highest recorded mileage that I have been able to prove is for a 1947 Hurricane (164346) which has now done 412,000 miles and still runs well.

The relatively high survival rate is yet another testimony to their staying power. Perhaps the fact that Armstrong Siddeley owners have been so well catered for with spares has helped the situation and kept cars on the road during their twilight period when they were neither considered modern enough for day to day use, nor old enough to be interesting and collectable. Their maintenance cost per mile is low which, coupled with a modest petrol thirst, makes for economic motoring, while depreciation is nonexistent if their use is sensible and worthwhile appreciation is more likely the rule.

3

Bright new jewel

The 346 Sapphire, 1952 to 1959
On October 8, 1952 the Armstrong Siddeley factory announced the Sapphire, an entirely new model from end to end. This car caused quite a sensation when it was launched, it was an immediate success and, once again, a great proportion of the early production was exported.

Very few cars were actually built in that late part of 1952, but it was a very different story in 1953, as the factory had begun to wind down the 18hp production line to make room for the growing demand from all over the world for the Sapphire. Reasonable output was achieved in the early part of 1953 and by mid 1953 almost all production effort went into the Sapphire, with 22 to 26 cars a week rolling out of the factory.

The Sapphire was named after the highly successful Sapphire jet aircraft engine and to further emphasize the link with modern aviation the designers saw fit to incorporate miniature jet engine pods on either side of a fairly futuristic sphinx bonnet mascot. The wisdom of this touch of flamboyance on a car of such restrained elegance has been questioned by many.

The designation 346 was not initially used; it was retrospectively introduced to avoid confusion with the smaller 234/236 Sapphires which were introduced in 1955. The logic behind the nomenclature was that the engine size was 3.4 litres and it had six cylinders. Interestingly, the original production drawings all refer to the car as a 340 model, with subsequent drawings entitled 346. The Mark 1 or Mark 2 description was also added afterwards to differentiate between the original model and the improved version introduced some two years later.

The Sapphire was a full six-seater car of fairly large dimensions and considerable refinement. The only styles initially available were a four-light or a six-light version of an otherwise identical saloon. A limousine body became available on a lengthened chassis in 1955 and proved popular mainly for formal work.

The Sapphire instantly became one of those cars that people aspired to own. It was considerably more costly than the 18hp range then being phased out, and in many ways established a new threshold for performance and quality from the factory. Some of the more staid Armstrong Siddeley owners saw the Sapphire as too expensive and too large, and felt they were not now being catered for, but such was its popularity that it created almost an entirely new market among discerning motorists. These people loved its 'highway eating' characteristics which combined with exceptional road holding to make it a car that was ideal to use for long trips. Even by the standards of the 1980s there are few cars so capable in this area, particularly if you fit your Sapphire with the modern radial tyres which were not available when it was produced.

The Sapphire was initially offered with an electrically controlled version of the four-speed preselective gearbox which was specially designed for it, with the change mechanism on the side rather than towards the top, making it more squat than any previous preselective unit. The car could also be obtained with an all synchromesh four-speed gearbox with the then-popular steering column gearlever. With the introduction of the Mark 2 model for 1955, an automatic version also became available. This used a four-speed gearbox of Rolls-Royce manufacture made under licence from General Motors and whilst successful in itself, stole some of the car's performance and sparkle.

The preselective gearbox was by far the most popular and in the writer's opinion by far the most desirable, but the other options opened up the market to cater for all tastes. As there were slightly more Mark 2 cars produced than Mark 1 and the automatic gearbox

1958 Sapphire 346 Mark 2, chassis number C347469, owned by W. Bladon. Though retaining styling links with traditional coach-built forms, the Sapphire was Armstrong Siddeley's first design to be conceived in the modern, full-width manner, without even vestigial running boards, and it was of pressed steel construction.

73

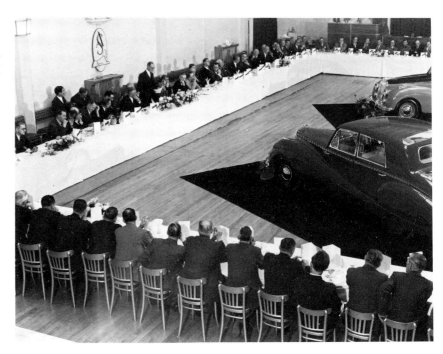

Official dinner to launch the all-new Sapphire model. The car was announced in both four-light and six-light forms, an example of the former being prominently displayed here.

was only available on the Mark 2, cars so fitted represented about half the series, leaving the balance divided into preselective and synchromesh models. It seems that the synchromesh gearbox always remained popular, while the automatic gearbox attracted many of the previous preselective buyers. The preselective Mark 2 car was the one produced in least numbers and is today by far the most coveted and sought after by enthusiasts. Quite a number of Mark 2 cars have been changed over to preselective in later life and even a few Mark 1 cars have been changed from synchromesh to preselective.

The Sapphire production ran from October 1952 to late 1958 for the saloons and from March 1955 to November 1959 for the long chassis limousines. Numbers produced were: Mark 1 (four or six-light bodies, saloon only) 3,750; (one Mark 1 Sapphire was exported CKD but was actually never assembled); Mark 2 (four or six-light saloon, limousine, and others) 3,947; total production, 7,697. Chassis numbers are: Mark 1, 340001 to 343750; Mark 2, 343751 to 347697.

The long wheel-base chassis has no separate numbering system unlike the 18hp and Star long chassis. The production of long-wheelbase chassis continued past the introduction of the Star saloon and was only discontinued when the Star limousine's introduction was imminent. Thus the last 53 chassis were all for limousines. The long-wheelbase (limousine) chassis had a number of obvious changes to accommodate the extra length and to deal with the extra weight (about 5cwt) – heavier duty brakes, wider wheels, increased rear track, etc. As with all previous chassis production, the factory batch ran each subseries and these batches are listed in Appendix 11 to help in understanding the various minor differences in cars from one batch to another. The ordering in of supplies was controlled by the batch build process.

The chassis frame

The main chassis frame is of box section fabricated steel pressings and varies in depth depending on areas of load. It tapers both to the front and rear, has a huge cross-bracing central member, and is further strengthened by two 2.5in diameter cross tubes and an elaborate but detachable front crossmember which carries the suspension.

The chassis is lighter than the 16/18hp frame but more robust and rigid, deflecting only one degree for a torsional load of 1,145lb ft. This frame is deliberately made very light in front of the front crossmember and behind the rear spring shackles to enable it to collapse progressively in the event of an accident yet not distort the main section. The mountings that carry the bumper bars are specially made to telescope on direct impact or break off sideways in a typical crossroads collision. This was very advanced thinking for 1952 and many owners have been very glad of this forethought in design: many a bad accident has not resulted in a bent or misaligned main chassis frame.

In service, this chassis has been almost totally trouble free. The only item giving any problem is the earlier front crossmember which has been occasionally known to crack when owners repeatedly drive their cars at high speed into bad potholes and unmade creek

1954 Sapphire Mark 1 undergoing final preparation before leaving the factory. The loving care lavished on these cars was an important factor in the high quality of finish which was obtained.

75

Factory photograph from 1952 of a Mark 1 Sapphire chassis. The robust central cruciform structure is evident, as are the front bumper mountings designed to collapse progressively on impact. The polished alloy finish for the rocker cover was only used on the first dozen or so cars.

crossings, particularly as in these situations the brakes are usually being used hard, minimizing available suspension travel. It is repeated actions of this nature that cause cracking; some cars have even been known to have the coil spring abutment tower punched out of the crossmember. A new crossmember fortunately can be easily fitted, but such abuse was surely never within the car's design criteria. However, it happened frequently enough for the factory to introduce during the later Mark 2 runs a stiffened crossmember and high tensile steel lower suspension wishbones in an effort to make the cars more nearly idiot proof.

So good was the basic chassis frame that even with so many Sapphires used in outback Australia I can never recall a single case needing any repairs other than following major collisions. The chassis flexed very little and so caused minimal problems with the body. It was a very advanced design, overcoming many of the problems associated with other separate chassis frames, and incorporated a lot of the engineering thought now applied in unitary construction cars.

The suspension and steering
Unlike the 16/18hp series with its torsion bars, the Sapphire featured a conventional coil spring and wishbone independent front suspension, the unequal length wishbones having a 25 degree trailing angle. The trailing effect was a typical W.O. Bentley engineering concept and reflects his involvement in the early Sapphire design. Girling telescopic shock absorbers were mounted concentrically within the springs. The length of the righthand spring was marginally longer than the lefthand to allow for the ever-present weight of a driver when the car was in use. The vertical suspension movement was controlled at the ends of its travel by rubber buffers which were made of variable resilience to ensure that

76

Front suspension of a Sapphire, in this case a Mark 2 model with 12in diameter trailing shoe brake, above on a bare chassis, with the anti-roll bar linkage in the foreground (the chain is supporting the chassis for photography, not standard equipment!) and left seen from underneath the car looking forwards.

a progressive rather than an abrupt bump stop action occurred.

The front wishbone pivot points were of three main types. The lower inner mountings were Metalastik rubber bushes, while the top inner had a long threaded adjustable shaft running in a bushed, threaded housing. The outer pivot points for the first 3,000 cars (to chassis 343000) were also screwed pins and bushes, but commencing at chassis 343001 these were changed to the Metalastik rubber type; this change marginally softened the ride and cut out four of the lubricating nipples.

The king pins were very long, forged steel pins which had an eye at the top for the outer upper suspension pivot, and ran in two bronze-faced steel bushes within the stub axle assembly. Hub bearings were Timken brand races of the roller type, two per side.

The steering linkage consisted of a centre idler connecting divided tie rods and the pitman arm from the steering box via a short drag link. The whole of the front suspension and steering linkage was lubricated with EP140 gear oil, not grease, being designed to store a certain amount of oil and let it through to the working surfaces as required. It should be noted by owners and service establishments that the use of grease only blocks the oil ways and starves the moving parts of lubrication, reducing the otherwise long life of the components to perhaps as little as 10,000 to 15,000 miles. Several owners wouldn't be told – often their service 'technician' was even less convinced – and for greasing their cars they paid the price rather dearly in repairs.

A rubber bushed front anti-roll bar was also fitted; this was mounted well forward and acted on the lower wishbone arms.

About halfway through the Mark 2 production run, the factory offered a power steering option. This was a ram system manufactured by Girling Ltd. It was unusual in providing the driver with a variable quadrant type control which regulated the amount of power boost to choice and made it possible to turn the boost effect off completely for high speed travelling.

The system had a rotary Hoburn Eaton pump, driven from a pulley on the crankshaft, delivering up to 650psi in pressure. The control mentioned was coupled by way of cable to a variable relief valve which altered the degree of boost delivered. The system worked well, but it did, however, enlarge the turning circle by approximately 10ft; apparently there was a fear that an ill informed driver might turn the steering wheel abruptly onto full lock and with too sharp an angle the car could be made to roll if travelling at high speed. Quite a lot of cars were fitted with this system and it has remained virtually trouble free in service except for the tendency to develop a knock at the sensing peg which could be heard rather than having any ill effect. A modification drawing was issued to overcome this irritating but insignificant problem.

It is not known precisely how many cars were supplied with power steering but at a guess at least 100 and probably more like 300. Unfortunately the loss of the individual files on so many Sapphires makes this information impossible to pinpoint accurately. Australia received 15 power steering Sapphires but I only know of two in New Zealand.

1955 Sapphire Mark 2 prototype undergoing testing on
the banked high-speed track
of the Motor Industry Re-
search Association (MIRA)
near Nuneaton. The car's
ability to sustain high cruising speeds was an important
product of development
work like this.

   The rear suspension was by semi-elliptic leaf springs working in a
conventional manner. The springs were quite long and relatively
flat; they allowed for a large amount of vertical travel. The forward
ends of the springs had Metalastik steel and rubber bushes, while at
the rear, at the spring shackle, the bushing was all rubber. There
were no radius rods or other location devices. The suspension was
controlled by tubular shock absorbers, normally of Girling
manufacture, heavily angled inwards. For those cars that had the
adjustable ride option, this feature consisted of a pair of Teleflow
variable valve shock absorbers controlled by long cables linked to an

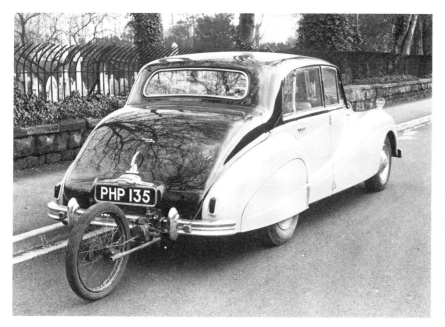

The Mark 2 prototype again,
with 'fifth wheel' fitted for
speedometer and perform-
ance checks. The position of
the script badge on the bootlid is non-standard, as are
the just visible fabricated
rubber stone guard on the
front of the rear wing and the
hubcaps of 18hp utility style
with Armstrong Siddeley inscription added.

79

adjusting wheel mounted beneath the instrument panel near the handbrake and within easy reach of the driver. The Sapphire was easy on shock absorbers: however, the adjustable ride type, being more complex, did not last quite as well as the simpler standard pattern.Cars and pick-ups destined for really rough conditions often had Armstrong heavy duty shock absorbers fitted. They are rather harsher in action and, while ideal for extremes in terrain, cause bodywork to become loose and rattly after some years of use. These shock absorbers are not a suitable substitute for general use. Now that roads in general are better throughout the world either original Girlings should be used as replacements or the Monroe-Wylie clone (110/659); the Sapphire also works very well on Koni shock absorbers, which are firmer but not too hard.

All Mark 1 cars and about half the Mark 2 cars also had a rear anti-roll bar fitted. This feature was deleted from chassis 343364, why I will never know! Many owners of later 346 Sapphires and quite a few Star Sapphires have had anti-roll bars fitted in later years, certainly highly desirable if you really like to drive your car. Late in the Mark 2 production run, commencing at chassis 346693, a new rear spring was introduced for normal issue. This lowered the car's tail marginally and featured two inverted leaves which only came into use when the spring was nearing the end of its upward travel. Some owners have mistakenly thought that these leaves were wrongly assembled and turned them upside down to make them look more like an earlier spring, thus hardening the ride and risking leaf breakage.

The brakes

During the life of the Sapphire there were two entirely different braking systems employed for the saloons as well as a heavy duty system for the limousine chassis.

The first 3,750 saloon cars (all the Mark 1 models) had a Girling hydraulic system that operated drums of 11in diameter and 2.25in width. The front brakes were the two leading shoe type (non self-adjusting) while the rear brakes had one leading and one trailing shoe, with a mechanical handbrake. There was no booster/servo. This system was quite successful for all normal use but lacked capacity for constant high speed use. There seems little doubt that the Armstrong Siddeley factory had little concept of the amount and frequency of high speed use so many of their cars were to be given by owners, particularly once the twin carburettor option became available. That made 100mph not only possible but used frequently by many, especially in countries with large distances to travel.

Thus at chassis 343751 for the Mark 2 series the brakes underwent a major revision: the brake drum diameters were increased to 12in, all front shoes became the trailing type and a large capacity Clayton Dewandre booster/servo was employed. The brake shoes carried some four square inches less in lining area (now 180sq in) but, more importantly, the new system allowed a greater cooling area per drum and the larger double finned drums allowed for much better heat dissipation.

This later system worked exceptionally well and brought the

Sapphire to the forefront in brakes for the era. This system today still acquits itself very nearly as well as the modern disc systems. Interestingly, the factory were working on disc brakes as early as 1955 and considered fitting them to the Monte Carlo rally cars, but they did not appear until the introduction of the Star Sapphire late in 1958.

The long-wheelbase models had a derivative of this Mark 2 system with bell shaped drums, larger wheel cylinders, etc, which proved well able to cope with the limousine's extra weight.

In all cases the handbrake was cable operated from a pistol grip underdash lever, working on both rear shoe sets. The handbrake in all cars worked well, which was essential as, with the preselective gearbox, there is no 'park' position as on an automatic, nor can it be left in gear as with a manual box. Once the engine is stopped, the Newton centrifugal clutch automatically disengages, breaking the coupling of the engine to the transmission.

Engine compartment of a Sapphire Mark 2, this example being fitted with the popular option of twin carburettors which provided a considerable increase in performance.

The engine

Like all previous Armstrong Siddeley designs but one, the Sapphire engine was an in-line six-cylinder unit, but at that point in the description most similarity, excepting engineering excellence, ceased. The engine was an entirely new design from end to end and was technically very up to date. It was a 'square' concept engine where the bore and stroke were identical dimensions of 90mm instead of the old long-stroke proportions, but the biggest change came in the arrangement of valves, combustion chambers and camshaft location. The Sapphire engine had an advanced head design, of crossflow type, where the inlet charge entered the engine on the righthand side and the exhaust gases were taken away on the lefthand side. The combustion chambers were of hemispherical form with one large inlet and one large exhaust valve per cylinder; these

81

Righthand side of a Sapphire 346 engine equipped for fitting to an automatic transmission Mark 2 car, with a single carburettor.

Lefthand side of a Sapphire engine, showing the two three-branch exhaust manifolds. This is again an automatic transmission version, this time with twin carburettors.

This engine has the carburettor linkage, petrol pipe layout and fan of an early Mark 1 car, and the bellhousing required for coupling to a preselective or synchromesh gearbox.

Righthand side of a twin-carburettor engine with changes to the carburettor linkage, petrol pipe, water pump and fan as installed in Mark 2 cars. The bellhousing is the automatic transmission type.

valves were steeply inclined and were operated through rockers on two parallel rocker shafts by angled pushrods from the camshaft which was high on the righthand side of the engine block.

This layout gave very nearly the same level of efficiency as a highly complex and much more costly double overhead camshaft engine. The factory had built at least two prototype twin overhead camshaft 3-litre engines (of W.O. Bentley design) but in testing had found problems in noise, especially with the 4.5ft-long timing chains. From what the writer has been able to research, the other reason, possibly the prime one, for not proceeding with this style of engine was the general worry about adequate servicing for such a unit, particularly in export markets. So they chose the wise compromise and managed to have nearly the same performance as a twin overhead camshaft unit but the servicing ease of a pushrod engine, so dealer concern and warranty problems were minimized with little loss of engine efficiency. This design was no doubt influenced by W.O. Bentley's consultancy at the factory, though Armstrong Siddeley Motors took full credit for the new engine, especially as it was so successful.

The Sapphire was introduced with a single DAV36 Stromberg carburettor. After some 500 cars had been built, a twin carburettor option was announced; again Stromberg carburettors were used, of the very similar DAA36 type. This gave a considerable lift in performance, raising the power of the engine from 125 bhp to 150bhp with virtually no increase in weight, thus lowering acceleration times. If the twin carburettors were used exactly as the single carburettor version there was a saving in fuel, too, but most owners who wanted the extra performance weren't very interested in a marginal improvement in economy. In both cases the induction manifolds were water jacketed to provide a 'hot spot' effect. To accommodate the twin carburettor option there was also a change to the rocker cover involving the repositioning of the filler neck and the provision for two sets of support brackets for the air cleaners.

For home deliveries the carburettors had single (or twin) large wire mesh air silencer/cleaners. For dusty export markets, single carburettor cars came with a very effective oil-bath type air cleaner. It was unfortunate that it was not possible in the space available under the bonnet to fit twin oil-bath air cleaners on twin carburettor cars. Anybody using a 346 Sapphire with a single carburettor in dusty conditions should ensure that they fit an oil-bath air cleaner as the saving in engine wear is very considerable. The writer, some years ago, learned from the Queensland dealers workshop manager of a Sapphire that was used in the desert areas of central Australia where the engine had advanced wear at 60,000 miles as it was a twin carburettor car (approximately 10% of all Sapphires arriving in Australia were of the twin carburettor type) yet a similar car with a single carburettor and an oil-bath air cleaner, used in much the same conditions, had only 0.001in bore wear after over 100,000 miles. Fortunately there are not too many situations existing today where excessive dust is such a problem, the last 30 years having seen vast improvements to roads all over the world.

All Sapphires have very similar exhaust systems, the only

variants being for cars fitted with automatic gearboxes and a longer intermediate pipe for long-chassis vehicles. The exhaust gases were taken from the engine by a pair of three-branch exhaust manifolds feeding through two downpipes into a single front collector box. From there a single intermediate pipe ran into the large rear silencer which was mounted forward of the petrol tank. From this silencer the gases were ducted away using a single tail pipe to emerge near the lefthand rear quarter of the car. The exhaust systems were supplied by the well known and respected Burgess company. This whole system, like that of the 16/18hp series, hung in figure-8 rubber bushed hangers which fully isolated it from both the chassis and the body. Mountings lasted very well, some cars still using the same today, even though they have probably had several silencer and pipe replacements in the many years of use. The Sappire with a genuine system is a very quiet car as far as the exhaust noise

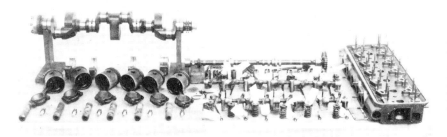

Components of a Sapphire engine laid out for inspection after durability testing. The broad cylinder head accommodated twin rocker shafts to operate inclined valves in the efficient hemispherical combustion chambers.

is concerned. Some cars that have been fitted with non-standard exhaust systems are quite noisy and non-original replacements have, in most cases, been found to be only marginally acceptable at the best.

The cylinder block and crankcase is a complex one-piece casting in iron, with generous water cooling passageways around the bores which are part of the casting and not separate liners. The crankshaft is massive and counterbalanced, running in four large bearings, the rear bearing being wider than the others to accommodate the weight of the flywheel. On the righthand side of the engine is situated the camshaft which also runs in four bearings of the Vandervell bimetal type; it has fairly radical cam profiles for this kind of car which give sporting characteristics to the engine and no doubt did much to give the Sapphire its brisk performance. The pistons are of Brico manufacture, in aluminium alloy, with a domed top, and equipped with three piston rings, the top one chrome faced and the bottom being an oil control ring. The bore/stroke ratio of 1:1 (square) keeps piston speeds to very acceptable levels: the critical figure of 2,500ft per minute piston speed, generally recognised as the limit for relatively low bore wear, is not reached until the vehicle is travelling at 86mph. Even in the wide open spaces of countries like Australia the proportion of constant use in excess of 86mph would not be all that great in most instances.

The pistons are connected to the crankshaft by H-section conrods and the specification called for extremely careful balancing: maximum variation between any two rods was set at plus or minus

Completed Sapphire 346 Mark 2 cars awaiting shipment from the factory in 1955. The finished cars are for local delivery while those with protected chrome, and bumpers and hubcaps not yet fitted, are destined for export.

2 drachms (a drachm is about the weight of the corner of a postage stamp!). The big ends are fitted with Vandervell bimetal bearings, while the little ends have bimetal bronze-faced bushes.

At the front of the motor is a fairly conventional layout with sprockets and timing chain used to drive the camshaft. The only unusual feature is an eccentric chain adjuster which can be operated quite easily by a person lying on his/her back under the front of the car. The system works very well and the only problem has been that, if neglected, the chain gradually stretches, becomes too loose and by lashing about can destroy the splines on the adjuster shaft and cause the external D-plate to become disconnected. This usually only means a lot of noise and mostly you are able to drive home rather than having to do a roadside repair. People rebuilding these engines are advised to use two D-plates, thus doubling the spline contact area, and by so doing all risk of possible future failure is removed. But this minor problem has only occurred at very high mileages or on engines that were badly neglected.

There is no harmonic balancer fitted as the engine was beautifully balanced in its manufacture. At the rear of the crankshaft is bolted one of three entirely different flywheels, to suit synchromesh, preselective or automatic gearbox applications. Both the synchromesh and preselective flywheels had shrunk on ring gears, but with the Rolls-Royce automatic gearbox this was not the case and this causes problems when the teeth become worn. The Australian company, Repco Limited, manufacture replacement ring gears for these automatic cars, shrink fitted in the usual way after the flywheel's periphery has been machined free of the worn teeth. The Repco part number is 388, and Repco also make ring gears for the other flywheels (part number 301).

The radiator was manufactured in copper and brass for Armstrong Siddeley by the Coventry Radiator Company and was of the vertical downflow type with a large header tank on the top. A tube through the base accommodated the starting handle, and the radiator could be drained with a simple tap on the bottom tank. The capacity of the radiator was quite sufficient even in very hot climates: overheating was not a problem unless the core was clogged or neglected or there was some other fault in the cooling system – in later years corroded water pump bodies are a main cause of overheating.

Mounted under the lefthand end of the header tank was an aluminium elbow that took the water delivery from the engine. In this elbow was housed an AC bellows thermostat. This arrangement was not ideal due to pressure and turbulence making the top hose life shorter than normal, dictating annual replacement. This was overcome with the Star Sapphire when the thermostat was mounted on the pump. The cooling system was pressurized at 4psi for the earlier cars, later increased to 7psi on later Mark 1 cars and all Mark 2. The radiator was fixed at the base with two long studs which had double rubber pads for insulation, and a pair of specially shaped moulded rubber pads held the top of the radiator in position and cushioned it from body movement. This system worked very well and gave the radiator a very long life: most Sapphires to this day still have their original radiator and in many cases the original core.

The transmission

The Sapphire was released initially with a choice of two gearboxes, an Armstrong Siddeley produced four-speed preselective with electric selection control and a four-speed all-synchromesh gearbox, with a column-mounted gearlever, which was purchased from Rootes Ltd. An automatic version followed for the Mark 2 cars, making the Sapphire the only car ever to be offered with the choice of three entirely different gearboxes. The automatic was also a four-speed model and, as already mentioned, was manufactured by Rolls-Royce under licence from General Motors. Of course, enthusiasts have their own opinions as to which gearbox is the best – so having owned and used all types, I must also have my vote, and I feel the preselective gearbox is by far the best, with the synchromesh as a good second choice. I feel the automatic is not as smooth as I would like and robs some of the car's peformance. It has rudely been referred to by some people as the 'jerkamatic'!

Turning first to the preselective box, about 4,000 Sapphires were built with this transmission and the greater number of these were of the Mark 1 chassis series or the Mark 2 long-wheelbase limousine chassis. The standard chassis Mark 2 saloon is relatively rare as a preselective car. Like previous Armstrong Siddeley preselective gearboxes, this one was also housed in a large cast aluminium case, but the design was modified to minimize height in an effort to have a relatively flat front floor. This was achieved by mounting the selectors, bus bar, pressure spring etc away from the top at approximately the 10 and 2 o'clock positions. This made the Sapphire preselective quite different in appearance to any previously produced preselective gearboxes but it did not alter its mechanical operation: on the lefthand side of the gearbox were externally mounted the five gear selection solenoids and a gearbox operating master switch, a first for Armstrong Siddeley. These components were so successful that a failure is almost unknown. Gear selection was by a remote control column-mounted miniature gate change that was, in fact, a multi-function switch which controlled the preselecting functions and operated the reverse light. The gearbox also featured a multi-disc clutch for the direct drive top gear in lieu of the earlier cone clutch – no doubt this change was required to enable the far greater power of the engine to be handled without problems. In front of this gearbox there was the usual centrifugally operated Newton dry plate disc clutch which functioned as a traffic clutch enabling the driver to stop the car by just using the brake pedal. The Newton clutch was designed to engage at 575rpm on all Sapphire models.

This form of transmission gave by far the most brisk performance and was generally almost entirely trouble free. The Newton clutch was, of course, a wearing part and needs overhaul about every 80,000 miles, depending upon traffic use, while most gearboxes will run to at least a quarter of a million miles before needing new bearings. The main drive train will normally last (assuming no abuse or lack of oil) for at least half a million miles, routine toggle action adjustments being very occasionally required. The biggest single problem with preselective gearbox cars is the need to keep the accelerator and carburettor linkage in top condition, as a worn or sloppy linkage means that you cannot control the progressive action of the Newton centrifugal clutch in a proper fashion, which results in rough take-offs from rest and, in extreme cases, breaks engine mounts. Some owners fail to look after this linkage, then complain about rough engagement of the clutch. It is important to ensure that all linkage is kept oiled and properly adjusted, and when it becomes worn all ball joints should be replaced.

About 1,650 Sapphires were fitted with ordinary manual transmission, fairly evenly spread through the whole of the production run, with perhaps a little bias towards the Mark 2 cars. Sapphires fitted with synchromesh gearboxes were about 4-5% cheaper than the preselective variant, which no doubt helped in some markets, particularly where imports were controlled in monetary quota terms rather than in numbers of cars. In Australia about 25% of all Sapphires were synchromesh cars, while for New Zealand the figure would be closer to 85%.

The synchromesh gearbox was manufactured by the Rootes Group and was also used in the Humber Snipe. It had a large cast iron case and provided four forward speeds, all with synchromesh engagement. The gear selection was by a steering column shift with a reverse gear safety lockout. This linkage was supplied by the Bloxwich company. The gearbox is remarkably satisfactory and almost never needs attention, the only normal problem being worn linkage on high mileage cars. A major linkage overhaul is recommended betwcen 100,000 and 150,000 miles, depending upon use. Column shifts were the accepted arrangement of the era, and though for a time a proprietary company offered a central floor shift conversion, how many owners, if any, fitted this is not known. The writer has never seen such an installation and cannot find anyone who has one fitted to a Sapphire, thus I am not prepared to make any comment about its operation, even though the idea sounds good. As the Sapphires have grown old, with, in most cases, high mileages being the order of the day, the synchromesh transmission has fallen from favour among enthusiasts, with many cars having been converted to preselective, probably mainly because of worn gear linkage rather than any real gearbox problems. I would suggest to owners of synchromesh cars that they fully overhaul the shift linkage and replace faulty and worn items, then they will find out just how satisfactory the gearboxes really are.

For the Mark 2 series a fully automatic gearbox became available. It was marketed as 'the two pedal control model' to avoid confusion with the preselective gearbox which had been marketed in the 1930s as 'the self-change gearbox' and the words 'Sapphire Automatic' were added in badge form to the boot lid, which was hardly consistent. This gearbox was fitted to just over 2,000 Sapphires, both saloons and limousines. The gearbox was purchased from Rolls-Royce Ltd and was unusual in as much as it was a four-speed system without the usual variable ratio intermediate gearing. The gearbox is still popular and, although rendered somewhat dated by newer designs, works well, though like all automatics it robs the car of a significant amount of acceleration. This unit when fitted to the Sapphire is not particularly smooth in operation but then with minimal hydraulic operational losses it doesn't have as much effect on fuel consumption as many of the smoother automatic gearboxes of today.

The serviceability of these automatic gearboxes is good but not outstanding; they seem to need minor overhauls (adjustments, new seals etc) from time to time, with major overhauls between 100,000 and 130,000 miles, depending upon use. Owners are advised to change the oil regularly and have adjustments done as recommended by the factory. In this way you will considerably lengthen the gearbox lifespan.

One curious feature is the non-provision of a PARK position on the selector quadrant. Instead, to secure a positive parking lock, you select reverse gear which automatically brings this function into operation once the engine is stationary. The gears are selected by a lefthand-mounted steering column quadrant which is very like the 16/18hp preselective gearbox quadrant. The gears are designated NEUTRAL, NORMAL (this equates to DRIVE in today's parlance), FAST (this holds third gear to just over 60mph, and re-engages it at the same speed as you slow down), FIXED SECOND (which will change back to first for full-throttle acceleration but won't change above second) and REVERSE. There is no opportunity to manually select the first gear ratio.

An inspection of the various ratios, listed in Appendix 9, is interesting and shows to some extent why the preselective gearbox cars have the best acceleration. The low second gear on the automatic gearbox does not serve these cars particularly well as there is too large a gap between it and third gear.

The Sapphire's drive is taken to the differential by an open two-piece propeller shaft assembly fitted with three universal joints, a centre bearing assembly and the usual spline. The front shaft is relatively short and has one universal joint at the gearbox coupling flange while at the other end it has a yoke and a Layrub central support bearing, with each end of the yoke carried in soft rubber bushes on special waisted mounting pins affixed to the cross bracing in the central chassis area. The rear shaft is longer and is fitted with front and rear universal joints and a sliding spline on the forward end. The whole assembly is of Hardy Spicer manufacture.

By fitting a two-piece driveshaft, it was possible to design a body with a flat rear compartment floor, and the elimination of the driveshaft tunnel made three abreast seating far more comfortable. There are three lengths of front driveshaft to accommodate the three gearbox options, and two lengths of rear shaft, one for the standard length chassis and one for the long or limousine chassis.

This driveshaft arrangement has proved entirely satisfactory and requires a minimal frequency of overhauls, generally at about 100,000 mile intervals. All service parts are readily available over the counter at most of the larger parts outlets or bearing shops.

Coming to the rear axle, again the factory chose to buy out and selected a differential from the Salisbury range. Initially these cars had the 2HA type differential which excepting the axle shaft length and the gear ratio was identical to that of the 16/18hp models. Commencing at chassis 340995 it was changed to the more modern and less bulky 4HA type. This unit has finer axle splines. In spite of the change, the standard gearing of 4.091:1 was maintained. Both differentials are very long lasting and almost trouble free, and in service generally remain untouched for at least 250,000 miles. A few owners specified a higher axle ratio and in these cases the 3.77:1 ratio crown wheel and pinion was fitted: this ratio was later standardized in the Star Sapphire which has a larger engine.

When the limousine or long chassis was developed, it was necessary to have a tougher differential, lower gearing and wider track. The choice was again from Salisbury and the type 5HA with its heavier duty construction was selected. The ratio for this differential is 4.451:1 which suits the heavier car. The limousines, because of the lower differential ratio and additional all-up weight do not have the top speed of the normal saloon, however they will comfortably exceed 90mph and seem almost as brisk to drive. A top speed of 95mph is close to that of the saloon model which will generally just exceed the magic 100mph figure. The only service problem after extensive use seems to be the occasional instance of a broken halfshaft which is, fortunately, relatively easily replaced, the writer actually having changed one on the roadside in a remote part of Tasmania some 1,000 miles from home.

Wheels, tyres and hubcaps
The Sapphire saloon was only offered with a standard five-stud, bolt-on, pressed steel disc wheel. There werc no significant changes to the wheels during the production run, although there are marginal differences between early and late cars. The wheel diameter is 16in

and the rim width 5.5in. These wheels are normally clad with a standard Dunlop tube tyre of 670x16 size. Radial tyres had not been released when the Sapphires were made. However, suitable radial tyres make dramatic improvements to the car's handling, wet weather grip and lightness of steering, and a great many Sapphires have been equipped with 185x16 or 205x16 radial tyres, the Pirelli brand being by far the most popular though owners in Australia are starting to equip their Sapphires with Nokia brand 205x16 tyres from Finland with remarkable success.

The standard Sapphire had three varieties of hubcaps during six years of manufacture. The first had a semi-dome type cap with straight pressed edges. The next issue commencing at chassis C342151 had a swaged edge for extra strength but was otherwise the same as the original issue. At about chassis C343050 (actual chassis number never recorded), the words 'Armstrong Siddeley' were also incorporated for the remaining Mark 1 Sapphires, all Mark 2 Sapphires and through to the end of the Star's production run.

When the factory developed the oil company pick-up (a heavy duty, short chassis truck for Middle Eastern and desert use), they fitted a variety of 15in wheels and tyres depending upon customer order. The tyre sizes used were 600x15, 700x15, 710x15 and 890x15. The wheels rims were 5.5in wide excepting those fitted with the 890 section tyres where 6in rims were used. Normally the pick-ups were not fitted with hubcaps.

The 710x15 tyres and appropriate wheels were also fitted to the one-off special utility long-chassis pick-up C347664 which, at the time of writing, is displayed by the Rolls Royce Heritage Trust.

Together with the other significant changes that were occasioned by the introduction of the limousine long chassis, came a change of wheels and hubcaps. The wheels were still five-stud fixing and 16in diameter but had wider stud facings, were heavier and slightly different in shape in the central region. These wheels were fitted with either 700x16 or 760x16 tyres. The hubcaps were a simple dome type the same as used on the 234/236 models. They too had the words 'Armstrong Siddeley' stamped in a ring near the centre. Once again the use of radial tyres was not a question at that time, but certainly today's 205 width radials make a great improvement to the car's handling and braking, and many have now been so fitted.

All cars were available with deep dress rings to improve the appearance of the wheels. Initially they were factory options but then were supplied for all automatic and limousine models and later (about mid 1956) became standard fitment for all 346 cars. There were two types used, the very well known Ace brand Rimbellisher and a different but very similar type made by Litelugs: in both cases they were screw-fixed from inside the wheel, thus becoming relatively thief proof, but a bit of a nuisance when modern tyre fitting machines are used, necessitating their removal to avoid dents during the fitting of new tyres.

The factory painted all wheels the same colour as the lower part of the car's body. The wheels were fine lined until chassis C346501, when the practice was abandoned with only marginal ill effect as the factory was shortly to standardize dress rings on all cars.

Mechanical modifications

The following table of chassis changes will give owners and service technicians an understanding of the progressive improvements that were incorporated and help when ordering or installing replacement parts. In each case the commencing chassis number is quoted.

340015 Aluminium polished cast rocker cover deleted in favour of double skinned insulated pressed steel rocker cover, reducing tappet noise and oil leakage.

340150 (approx) to **34045** (approx) Engines numbered 340001 to 340164 had 6.5:1 compression ratio. However, some export cars had 6.9:1, and some 7.0:1. Compression ratio changed by piston fitment. Engines numbered 340431 onwards had 7.0:1 compression ratio, excepting special high performance engines which had ratios as high as 9.5:1.

340306 Steering centre idler stiffened.

340600 (approx) in June 1953: Twin carburettors became available as an option. Two Stromberg DAA36 in lieu of single Stromberg DAV36. Also available for retrospective fitting to earlier cars, a popular option.

340751 to **343751** Cable operated accelerator pedal linkage fitted in lieu of rod operation. Not an improvement, with many later cars being converted to the earlier arrangement once the cable became worn.

340995 Salisbury 2HA type differential replaced by Salisbury 4HA type: axle shafts for the 4HA unit have finer splined ends. An original spares list stated the change occurred at chassis 341000, but is incorrect and was later amended to 340995.

341250 Rear spring gaiters deleted as large spring deflections caused water entry and build up, which damaged springs rather than protecting them. The rough going in countries like Australia very soon proved the wisdom of this change, with most earlier cars having long since had their gaiters removed.

341251 Horns moved to inside engine bay, to prevent water damage in fording creek crossings, for export cars: by chassis 341537 all cars leaving the factory were so modified with dealers being requested to change retrospectively all earlier cars.

341500 Rear springs changed to lower rear end of car, new springs being part number EN61460 for UK delivery and EN61464 for export.

341523 Clutch and gear change pedal operating rod ends changed from two righthand threads to a right and a lefthand thread for easy adjustment.

341614 Rear engine mounting towers changed to avoid welded top section which sometimes failed at the weld.

341772 Rear brake cylinder diameter decreased by 0.125in to increase the proportion of rear braking (Diameter now 1.125in.)

342125 Hubcaps modified to incorporate swageing around edge for stiffening. Factory instructed all dealers to supply replacements in sets of four as early hubcaps had been known to suffer small fatigue cracks at the edge if cars were constantly used on unmade roads.

343000 On synchromesh gearbox cars the reverse light switch and trip mechanism totally redesigned and repositioned.

343000 Rubber bushes replaced metal screwed bushes in upper and lower outer front suspension wishbone pivot points: ride marginally improved and replacement costs slashed, unfortunately eliminating one of the steering geometry adjustment points.

343000 Preselective gearbox bell housing modified to improve gearbox pump.

343050 (approx) Hubcaps again marginally changed to incorporate the inscription 'Armstrong Siddeley' which was pressed into the centre dome section. Part number now EN62780.

343250 Water pump body slightly modified to improve water flow.

343501 Water pump body further modified to include a position for the temperature gauge sender: this pump body now standardized for all the remaining Mark 1 Sapphires, Mark 2s, Star Sapphires and 234s.

343501 Radiator header tank modified to delete the position for the temperature gauge sender. This radiator standardized for all Mark 2 Sapphires.

343501 Radiator cap pressure increased from 4psi to 7psi. This also standardized to the Mark 2.

343751 Mark 2 version announced late 1954. The Mark 2 cars incorporated a number of significant changes to both chassis and bodywork, principal amoung which were: (**a**) Full new braking system, drum diameters increased from 11in to 12in and finned for cooling. Vacuum servo by Clayton Dewandre used to allow an all-trailing-shoe system to be incorporated. (**b**) Accelerator became the organ pedal type with various linkage modifications. (**c**) Winking direction indicator lights became standardized for all markets. (**d**) Warning lights for hand brake, choke, winkers and high beam were incorporated. (**e**) Instruments changed to larger diameter and lit by ultraviolet light, cluster of three instruments changed to a cluster of four instruments, eliminating the separate ammeter. (**f**) Automatic gearbox became available, making a choice of three gearboxes to suit all customer tastes. (**g**) Handbrake mounting changed in detail for easier use. (**h**) Sphinx motif added to horn button, but not universally fitted at first. (**i**) Lobes added to heater and wiper switch knobs, and later also added to headlight switch knob. (**j**) Scuttle modified for automatic gearbox cars only, this modification standardized after existing stock used up. (**k**) Windscreen washers added and standardized, Trico A800 series.

344251 One-piece drag link introduced.

344501 Rear engine mountings further strengthened and heavier duty front engine mounting rubber used.

345364 Rear anti-roll bar deleted.

345633 New pitman arm introduced: has an A suffix part number and dealers were told to retrospectively fit the new arm to all earlier cars as a couple of failures had occurred. All owners are advised to ensure that their car's pitman arm has been changed – this is the only *essential* change of all the modifications introduced.

345653 First long-wheelbase chassis introduced for a production limousine.

346100 (approx) In November 1955 three new options became available: (**a**) Power steering of the Girling ram type became available. This featured adjustable boost by way of an instrument panel mounted quadrant which balanced the choke quadrant on the other side of the steering column. The power steering also meant a change in engine sump profile to accommodate the power ram. The earlier pattern power steering sump was an alloy casting, with a modified steel pressing used later. (**b**) Adjustable ride rear shock absorbers by Teleflow, the adjustment control being a large turn knob positioned near the handbrake lever. (**c**) Power windows, firstly by twin button control and later by two-way switch. The factory also offered these extras as a fitted option for earlier cars.

346501 High tensile steel lower wishbone arms for front suspension introduced.

346501 Stub axle assemblies modified to incorporate an O-ring lower king pin seal in lieu of the external seal.

346693 New rear springs introduced which had two override lower leaves, curved downwards.

347001 Oil sump changed to new pressing for universal application.

347297 Major change to brakes to bring car up to latest technology. This included different shoes, anti-rattle pads, new cylinders, etc: also Girling servo replaced Clayton Dewandre unit. (Most

Australian cars are now fitted with Repco/PBR type VH40 boosters which are an ideal modern replacement.)

347401 Synchromesh gearbox selector rod modified for better shift action.

Bodywork
Of the 7,697 Sapphire chassis produced, by far the largest number were fitted with the factory-built six-light saloon body. A number of standard chassis carried the alternative four-light saloon style. The long-wheelbase chassis were mostly equipped with limousine bodies. Completing the total were a short production run of pick-up trucks and a number of chassis fitted with special bodies by various coachbuilders.

All Sapphire body numbers commenced with the prefix number 25. The next number in the sequence is a figure between 1 and 6 which denotes the type of body, while the final four numbers denote the individual body within the series. The body numbering series, like that of the chassis, continued without interruption when the Mark 2 was brought into production.

Body type 25/1 was the six-light saloon, of which 6,896 were built. That total includes 49 cars assembled by Liberty SA in Belgium from CKD kits (chassis numbers recorded in Appendix 12); the remainder were built at the Armstrong Siddeley factory. Type 25/2 was the four-light saloon, total production 381. The next designation, 25/3, was applied to a special touring limousine built at the factory on a

The four-light body style was introduced alongside the six-light version but was destined to be built in much smaller numbers, a reflection, presumably, of customers' preferences. This is a factory photograph from 1952 of the first body of this type, number 25/2/0001, on chassis number C340004.

1954 Sapphire Mark 1, chassis C342943, owner W.P. Bradly, fitted with winkers and with Australian produced dress rings on the wheels.

standard-length Mark 1 chassis: it remained a one-off and the idea was not pursued. 25/4 was the long-chassis limousine, of which 381 were built. Type 25/5 was applied to 19 bodies provided by other coachbuilders for special purposes, most numerous among them being 14 hearses. 25/6 was the oil company pick-up truck, of which more anon, total production 45. Completing the total of 7,697 Sapphire chassis was one car supplied in CKD form to Buckle Motors in Australia and never assembled by them.

The design and construction of the Sapphire body was a significant step forward. The body was the first of the full width concepts by Armstrong Siddeley; gone were the traditional running boards that had served the marque since the birth of the motor car. Not only was the Sapphire an entirely new chassis but the body created for it was, in the eyes of its admirers, one of the most beautiful of all time.

1956 Sapphire Mark 2, chassis C346263, owner D. Hills: this is one of the few cars comprehensively fitted with optional extras to reach Australia, a less lavish level of equipment being more usual for export markets.

The Sapphire's body was of pressed steel construction, assembled in the Armstrong Siddeley body factory at Coventry. There was minimal structural woodwork in the body which was a great advantage in countries of high rainfalls, high temperatures and poor roads as wood rot and rattles were largely eliminated. The only woodwork of the non-ornamental type was in the edge areas of the turret around the rear quarter window and the shaped piece at the top of each door. These wooden components had a very modest amount of structural work to do and would seem to have been fitted as much to facilitate fastening the headlining as for any other purpose. Perhaps the factory could not quite escape the fifty-year tradition in the use of wood!

The body was designed for hand assembly and easy panel replacement in the event of an accident. The body had its own

This 1955 Sapphire, chassis C343910, owner P. Chesney, is an early Mark 2 car with preselective gearbox. Two-tone paintwork, with the darker colour on the upper part, complements the Sapphire's flowing lines well.

This close-up of a 1955 Mark 2, chassis C344668, owner K.H. McMinn, shows the details of the correct backing plate for the front registration number. This car also has the Lucas PL headlamps normally fitted to 1960 Star Sapphires.

This is the instrument panel of a Mark 1 model, as fitted to the 1954 Sapphire, chassis C341990, of Brian Castle.

On the Mark 2 panel, the ammeter is incorporated in the righthand multi-instrument dial. With the HMV radio installed, the heater controls are moved down below the panel in an additional walnut-finished mounting. This superbly preserved high-mileage car is chassis C343837, with pre-selective gearbox, owners Messrs Donaldson and Culgoa.

separate frame rails of substantial steel box section mounted onto the main chassis outrigger brackets. From these two rails were erected the turret, floor, and tail section which was welded into place at the rear, thus making the main composite structure. The only fixed points were the abutments of the rear wheelarches to the body members, the centre door posts and the windscreen posts being bolted to the body members and fully adjustable. The body assembler started by fitting the rear doors and aligned them with the rear wheelarches for an accurate and even gap, then adjusted the centre door posts to suit the door. He then hung the front doors to the centre post, firstly adjusting each to suit the rear doors, then adjusting the front part of the turret and scuttle to align with the door and again provide the required gaps. The front mudguards were then offered up to the scuttle sides and front doors, and also aligned. In this manner all the main panels are able to be accurately fitted. The rear mudguards were also adjustable in their fit to the rear wheelarch, and were only finally bolted up when the rear wheel spat aligned with the door and mudguard opening accurately. The bonnet, boot lid, radiator grille, and front bumper apron (often called the gravel tray) were also fully adjustable, making it possible to assemble the whole body to very tight gaps and tolerances. This is one of the real plus factors for the enthusiast restorer; there are few other bodies that offer such ease of adjustment.

The Sapphire body has proven itself to be very robust and quite a considerable number have been rebuilt after colossal accidents, where more importantly the occupants were kept remarkably safe and largely uninjured. Having been closely involved with Armstrong Siddeley cars for 35 years, the writer has never known of anyone killed in an accident with a Sapphire, or, for that matter, any other Armstrong Siddeley model. A beautiful four-light Sapphire was rolled end over end twice and was still capable of being driven home some 60 miles and later some 250 miles for repair.

Such ruggedness meant that the Sapphire body lasted remarkably well in hard use. There were the odd spots of weakness that became apparent in the high mileage cars, particularly those used in the rough outback, but the falling-to-pieces syndrome of so many European cars of the era was not evident in the Sapphire. Perhaps the best statistic to evidence this factor is that out of almost 400 cars that came to Australia, about 70% are still in serviceable condition or being restored, and a large proportion of these are in good to outstanding order, yet there would not be many that have not done at least 200,000 miles! Some Sapphires have reached over the half-million-mile goal.

Rust *was* a problem in some countries and it afflicted the Sapphire body without discrimination, particularly if salty mud was allowed to remain stuck to panels and under mudguard areas. However the

This factory shot of the controls of a 1955 Mark 2 Sapphire shows the heater quadrant mounted in the main panel, in the absence of a radio, and the four warning lights in the centre of the instrument cluster below the clock.

Sapphire faired no worse than other cars, and due to other excellent properties that the model offered, the cars were not scrapped in the quantity that some competitors were. Ironically, this means that rusty examples still exist, causing many people to comment about the rust when they see a poor or shabby Sapphire, whereas the comment should perhaps be directed towards the overall durability of the car, without which the rust would not be still on view!

As already mentioned, the Sapphire was made in two series (Mark 1 and Mark 2) and while there were many minor modifications, the body remained basically unchanged during its six-year production run, indicating the 'right first time' success of the design. The four-light body has proven itself if anything to be marginally stronger than the more popular six-light version.

The body was meticulously finished with lead wiping in complex areas such as at the foot of the windscreen posts and the blending of the roof gutters into the body at each end. The car was sprayed in nitrocellulose paint, being hand rubbed down between coats. The under mudguard areas and door interiors were frequently coated with a bituminous anti-drum protective coat, but strangely enough not all cars were so treated: this practice was not common when the Sapphire was in production and possibly was deleted by customer demand or it may have been related to the operating conditions that the individual car was expected to endure.

With the exception of the heavy pressed steel bumper bars and overriders, all other chromework was based on brass (or die-cast alloy in the case of the door handles and mascot). The extensive use of brass for items like the radiator grille, window frames and hubcaps made deterioration very slow, with most of these parts on many Sapphires still untouched some 30 or so years later.

The rear mudguards and front bumper apron were bolted to the main body and had plastic piping especially made to match either the paintwork, or occasionally the car's seat upholstery, or its fine lining. This is just another touch of quality that so often goes unnoticed.

The interior of the bodywork was very roomy and lavishly fitted out with genuine leather seats, pile carpet, nylon (ivory) headlining and, to complete the picture, ornamental walnut woodwork was used extensively.

The seats were very deeply padded, with both front and rear seats having central arm rests, and provided sumptuous comfort for long distance travel doing much to minimize passenger fatigue. So thoroughly was the leatherwork executed that each individual pleat was anchored by hand sewing back to the frame so it would not move. The cars were mostly fitted with a bench front seat but bucket seats were an option though few cars were so equipped, for the vogue in the 1950's was away from bucket seats. In Australia, not one single dealer order was with bucket seats! In most cases the seats had contrasting piping which added life to the interior, but this practice was thought a little radical at that time and quite a number of cars were ordered with self coloured piping to suit the conservative buyer.

The doors were trimmed in a most elaborate fashion with quite complex hand-made lining panels. In each door lining there was a very useful pocket which was covered with a spring loaded padded flap. In the front doors the pockets were so huge, due to the curvature of the door, that you could put up to four bottles of wine into one pocket and still shut the flap. In cars fitted with power windows, it was necessary to delete the rear door pockets to leave room for the mechanism, but not those in front which remained.

The interior was adorned with most attractive and elaborate polished walnut ornamental woodwork. All the main pieces had burr walnut veneer applied to their feature surfaces, this veneer being bookleaf matched side to side. The woodwork was of a very high

101

Split bench front seat with Radford conversion providing reclining backrests fitted to a 1957 Mark 2 Sapphire, body 25/4/0377, chassis C347304, owner D. Lomax.

Twin bucket seats in a 1956 Mark 2, chassis C346741, owner Miss E. Montgomery. This option is quite rare as only a few examples were built to this specification.

standard in quality and finish. There are 29 individual pieces of polished woodwork in a six-light Sapphire saloon. Each piece was individually fitted and no two cars were identical: there was a great variety of pattern in veneer from one car to another, with each car having an integrated set of woodwork.

The floor was covered with a plain synthetic velvet pile carpet: initially all cars were fitted with a pale fawn or camel colour but about two-thirds of the way through the Mark 1 production run (at about chassis C342600) the carpet colour was changed so that it matched the leatherwork as had been the practice with 16/18hp models. Most earlier Mark 1 Sapphires that have been recarpeted have adopted the later practice as the pale fawn carpet tended to be

Four-light Sapphires had this pocketed blanking panel inside the rear quarter. Optional sun roof and 234/236 style interior light are original equipment on chassis C347304.

easily soiled. Initially these carpets were edged in vinyl to match the seats but very early the factory changed to using a type of braid edging, which generally matched the carpet colour. Occasionally, if the carpets were of a very pale colour, they were edged in a contrasting darker colour, mostly picking up the piping colour in the seats. Beneath the carpets was heavy underfelt and in the Mark 2 cars there was a black paper/felt floor overlay as well, to help reduce noise. The carpets were secured with press fasteners along their edges, except at the scuttle where they were anchored with brewsters buttons on all but the early Mark 1 cars in which an expanding pin anchorage had proved not to be up to the job.

The interior had many other nice details such as grab handles on door posts for passengers, an underdash map reading light, a vanity mirror, and so on. If the body were of the four-light design, there were also special cubby boxes in the blanked off rear panel. The overall appearance of the interior was enhanced by a lightly ribbed ivory

'Panic strap' for rear passengers was available to order on saloons, though standard issue on limousine bodies. Fitting involved reinforcing the roof frame.

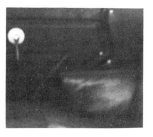

Rear interior of Sapphire Mark 2, chassis C346337, showing self-coloured piping trim and the usual arm rest shape.

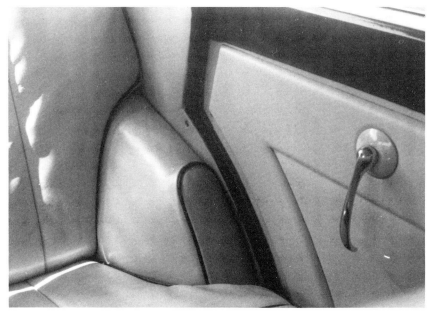

Inside the rear compartment of a 1958 Mark 2 car, with piping in a contrasting colour and the cut-back arm rest fitted to the last batch of Sapphires. Chassis C347469, owner W. Bladon.

Inside the boot of a 346 Sapphire, showing the spare wheel and pull-out tool tray stowed below the main boot floor. This is the plainest and most austere of a number of different trim styles applied to the boot, some cars leaving the factory with a fully carpeted luggage compartment.

synthetic headlining which gave the interior a spacious appearance. Cloth headlinings could be specified but seemed to have been rarely fitted, except to some limousines.

The boot area was another part of the body that warranted special attention, its shape and layout being very well designed. It had 16 cubic feet of usable space and was designed with a flat floor to accommodate two very large suitcases and three medium sized suitcases with the bulge in the bootlid allowing for suitcases to be carried vertically if required. Beneath the main boot floor was a stowage space for the spare wheel which enabled access to the wheel without needing to disturb the luggage, and beside the wheel was a separate compartment fitted with a rubber nest tool drawer containing a reasonable selection of high quality tools. Underneath the tool drawer the space was devoted to mounting the jack, while beneath the spare wheel in the trough of the beaver tail was mounted a Sutty brand tyre foot pump. This lower area also offered additional usable space for carrying items of a less bulky nature. The whole of the lower level of the boot was finished in paintwork which matched the top exterior colour of the car's paintwork, while the main boot area was finished off in an extraordinary variety of ways, and seems to have been trimmed to suit customer or dealer orders as there is absolutely no continuity from car to car. A number of different trimming materials were used at different times on the floor and sides of the boot; by no means the same material was always chosen

104

Examples of Sapphire boot trim combinations		
Chassis number	*Floor*	*Sides*
343040	Black rubber	Black paint
343910	Black wicker-work without edging	Black paint
340574	Black wicker-work with sewn edging	Black paint
340570	Black wicker-work without edging	Black wicker-work without edging
341131	Black wicker-work with sewn edging	Black wicker-work without edging
344667	Black wicker-work with sewn edging	Black wicker-work with sewn edging
341260	Black wicker-work with sewn edging	Brown ribbed composite
340990	Black wicker-work without edging	Fawn carpet without edging
340794	Carpet, edged, matching interior	Carpet, edged, matching interior

for both sides and floor of the boot of each individual car, and almost all the possible permutations seem to have cropped up at some point in production. A black composite material embossed with a wicker-work pattern was used, with or without sewn edging, for sides and floors, as was edged carpet (mostly matched in colour to the interior of the car). Black rubber matting was sometimes used on floors only. Other finishes sometimes used on sides only were black paint, a thin brown ribbed composite material, and unedged carpet (mostly fawn in colour). Almost all the cars delivered new in the UK and subsequently brought to Australia had a fairly austere combination, unedged black wicker-work composite on the floor and black painted sides. Other cars varied according to the importing dealer, but the commonest arrangement in Australia has the black wicker-work, with edging, on both sides and floor. The only other area of the body to consider is the engine compartment and this is finished in paintwork to match the exterior of the top half of the car.

The factory selected a range of colours and offered that any two could be used in a two-tone scheme. The colours were very well selected and did much to enhance the cars' appearance. As the body had a perfect line for breaking the colours, most two-tone schemes worked very well, and generally speaking the darker colour looks better on the top. The exceptions are Langham Grey with Corinthian Green, and Sand with Sable, perhaps because those colours are more toning than contrasting. The colour range was: Gazelle Fawn (mid fawn with a red tinge); Elephant Grey (dark grey with a blue tinge); Silver Grey (light grey with a distinct blue tinge); Langham Grey (light grey with a distinct green tinge, often referred to as pale green); Corinthian Green (dark green but stronger than British Racing Green); Dark Blue (almost navy); Sapphire Blue (very strong mid blue similar to the background colour on the car's badges); Pearl Grey (light fawnish grey, introduced in 1956); Ivory (soft pale cream); Black. In all cases the interior trim was a combination of leather for the seats and arm rests, with ICI vinyl closely matching the leather on the door trims and the back of the front seat.

There were a number of factory extras available on these cars, some of which have already been mentioned. The list was: (a) Wing mirrors (convex type), either Lucas or Wingard brand, for preselective and synchromesh gearbox cars, but standard equipment on automatic cars and all limousines; (b) Wheel dress rings or Rimbellishers; (c) Chrome exhaust pipe end, again optional on preselective and synchromesh cars and standard issue on automatic and limousines; (d) Radio – the approved extra was the Smiths Radiomobile/HMV with roof aerial. When the radio was fitted the heater quadrant was moved out of the instrument panel and centrally mounted beneath. To make this installation look pleasant to the eye, the correct additional fitting was an embellisher for this quadrant, mostly in polished wood to match the rest of the car's interior. In some cases a rear speaker was also specified which had a fader balance control. Most export cars were not equipped with the standard radio due to tariff and import restrictions, which resulted in all manner of local radios being fitted. (e) Power windows. These became an option for 1956 cars and were initially fitted with individual chrome plated push buttons, but later the more modern two way-switch was adopted. (f) Cigar lighter. This was not infrequently requested and if fitted by the factory was positioned on the instrument panel near the speaker grille, midway between the speedo, but it always looked an afterthought. (g) Panic straps for rear passengers. These were standard issue on the limousines but were fitted by the factory when requested for some 346 saloons. When this installation was specified, the roof edge frame was stiffened to provide a durable mounting prior to fitment of the headlining. (h) Windscreen washers on Mark 1 cars: these became standard issue on Mark 2 cars – brand being Trico, vacuum operated. (i) Dipping rear view mirror. Frequently the Lucas brand mirror was ordered in lieu of the small Wingard convex mirror. In addition to this list of factory extras, there were also a variety of dealer extras, particularly to tailor cars to local conditions in export markets. For example: (a) Tow bar. (b) Rear window venetian blind. (c) Canvas side window awning blinds (for use only when stationary). (d) Sun hood above windscreen (also factory fitted for some middle eastern exports). (e) Narrow type wheel dress rings. (f) Spat stoneguards mostly in stainless steel (Mark 1 cars only – rubber guards became standardized for Mark 2 cars). (g) Rear bumper bar overrider

protection inserts (invisible from outside) to prevent airborne stones travelling around inside and peppering the bootlid paint. (**h**) Petrol tank stoneguards for outback use. (**j**) Driver's door wind deflector. (**k**) Mudflaps.

Readers should also be aware that the factory would tailor a car to suit a specific customer especially in the area of colour schemes. However, as most cars were dealer ordered for stock rather than customer specials this only happened infrequently. Beyond the lists of add-on items already discussed there were a number of other alternatives available, specially built. For example, the Harold Radford Countryman conversions, executed on at least six Sapphires, included: (**a**) Camping body with seat arrangements convertible for sleeping; station wagon style fold down back seat plus lay-back front seats. (**b**) Boot picnic tables, being pull out type with towel rail and fold up mirror. (**c**) Special sphinx mascot. (**d**) More luxurious interior trim and appointments. (**e**) Sunshine roof. (**f**) Retractable picnic tables in the back of the front seats. (**g**) Divided front bench seat.

Appleyards of Leeds converted at least one if not two standard six-

This photograph of a very early Mark 1 Sapphire has been heavily retouched to show how a station wagon version might look. It is believed to have been discussed with Hoopers in response to a specific customer enquiry, but the outcome of the project is unknown.

This station wagon, however, definitely was built, by Appleyards of Leeds on a 1957 Mark 2 chassis, C347063, registered SWY 889, and it is thought that there was a second example as well, though the fate or whereabouts of either are unknown.

Three views of a 1953 Sapphire Mark 1, chassis C340426, with utility body by Coachcraft of Brisbane. In the lower photo it is seen earning its keep carrying a huge player piano in outback Australia in 1979, at which time its mileage was about 485,000! Note the condition of the so-called road.

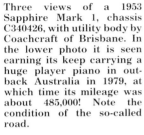

Quite a conversion! This Sapphire tow-truck, working at a garage in Preston, was concocted from two accident damaged cars. Owner D. Lomax.

light cars into station wagons – an extremely attractive conversion. It is also believed that another English coachbuilder built a similar station wagon, but no trace seems available. One shooting brake is known to exist, executed on a long-wheelbase chassis and presently undergoing restoration. Little is known about this vehicle and it is thought to be the only one.

The one-off touring limousine was a special Armstrong Siddeley-built saloon with the limousine-style glass division but no occasional seats, on the standard length chassis. In addition, the factory

108

Three special bodies on the long-wheelbase chassis. Above left is the one-off pick-up on chassis C347664 delivered on October 10, 1959 to Adcock & Shipley as a mobile display unit for their machinery, for which purpose it was originally fitted with a huge perspex dome. Preserved by the Rolls-Royce Heritage Trust, it is seen here in use by the Armstrong Siddeley Owners Club. Above is a station wagon with traditional wooden framing, offered for sale when new by Reigate Garage Ltd in April 1958 and currently undergoing restoration. Left, one of a small number of ambulances built on the 346: this example is chassis C347296.

allocated 18 chassis to coachbuilders for special body orders comprising three ambulances, 14 hearses, and a utility pickup. One further chassis was supplied to the coachbuilders Hooper & Co who built a luxury body for the Ameer of Bahawalpar in Pakistan.

Five prototypes of the Sapphire were known to exist. These were not generally sold by the Armstrong Siddeley factory but instead were allocated to senior staff who used them extensively to the end of their normal useful life. For example, one of the two early 346 prototypes with the 3-litre twin overhead camshaft W.O. Bentley engine was used by the late Mr Selwyn Sharpe until 1960 and covered almost a quarter of a million miles before being replaced by the Star Sapphire. (Armstrong Siddeley owners of long standing will well remember the wonderful and helpful letters Selwyn Sharpe wrote to owners around the world). Another prototype was a very unusual car known as a 340 Sapphire which had a full-width body of rather rounded lines and a Whitley style radiator grille.

One other vehicle which might have led to other things was a most attractive drophead coupe converted from a standard saloon by Minerva of Belgium and delivered on January 12, 1954 having taken 10 months to build. The chassis was number 340081, an early B batch car. This is believed to have been an unsuccessful conversion in spite of its stunning looks, for apparently the body lacked structural integrity. The car is thought to have been broken up many years ago, and in spite of considerable efforts by the Dutch Armstrong Siddeley club members, no trace has been found.

Bodywork modifications

In listing bodywork changes and modifications it is not generally possible to quote a chassis number for their introduction. There is no record relating chassis numbering back to body numbers nor is there a record of exactly where these changes occurred except for the major revisions for the introduction of the Mark 2. Most of these listed changes occurred at a specific non-recorded body number rather than at a chassis number. This was confused by the practice of batch running four and six-light bodies and batch running each paint/trim combination: these bodies were then fitted to chassis as the demand existed at that moment in production. Thus body numbers, while generally more or less following chassis numbers, in no way precisely followed from car to car and were often significantly out of step. For example, chassis 341067 (the 1,067th chassis) had a six-light body 25/1/0957 (the 957th six-light body), while the very next chassis 341068 also had a six-light body but numbered 25/1/0716, some 241 bodies earlier. The production run then reverted to the more normal practice of more or less coinciding, with chassis 341070 having body 25/1/0962, close to the first example but not absolutely in sequence. Thus the chassis number I have chosen for each of the following changes should be taken as a close approximation only of the starting point.

340025 Speaker grille in instrument panel made slightly smaller.

340050 One-piece front seat assembly of the bench type, changed from the late Whitley style, with new cushions, squab and frame. Separate cushion with vinyl covered rounded metal corner/ends, together with introduction of metal pan to seat frame. This allowed more padding and a more comfortable seat, while the squab was modified to provide curved back rests.

340066 (body 25/1/0065) Rear quarter window lower front corner was rounded and rear door window chrome frame modified to suit. This occurred on six-light bodies only, and resulted in the rear door chrome frame becoming common for both four and six-light bodies.

340100 Data plate showing chassis and body numbers together with lubrication schedule moved from bulkhead beneath the battery to side of engine bay on inner lefthand side of front mudguard panel.

340100 (first 100 bodies) Bonnet release cable: full length outer bowden deleted, replaced by a guide to minimize friction.

340200 Roof gutter front end at bottom of screen post now lead wiped into scuttle making it no longer appear to be a separate item.

340251 Twin side coach lines changed to a single coach line.

340400 to **340800** Speedometer changes: Mark 1 speedometers came in imperial or metric units and were produced within those two categories in three types. *First type*: used up to about chassis 340450, these speedometers were calibrated only to l00mph (or 160kph) in increments of 10. *Second type*: used sporadically from about chassis 340400 to about chassis 340800, these speedometers were calibrated to 120mph (or 200kph) in increments of 20. *Third type*: used sporadically from about chassis 340450 to about chassis 340800 then at about chassis 340800 became standardized, these speedometers were calibrated to 120mph (or 200kph) in increments of 10. In all cases the general appearance of the instruments was similar and the cases identical.

341000 Bootlid centre vertical chrome strip deleted, with the visual effect of reducing the apparent height of the car. This occurred after the first 1,000 bodies were built, but with the low production of four-light bodies this feature persisted as late as chassis 341097 at least.

341100 Front floor pan slightly changed to a universal type suiting both synchromesh and preselective gearbox shape (this occurred after the first 1,100 bodies were built).

341251 Centre radiator grille bar changed to a less prominent type, this gave better air flow characteristics. The change was done by putting two extra folds into the pressing of the centre bar.

341330 Glove box lock deleted except to special order – this continued to end of Mark 2 series.

341500 Front seat again changed, deleting metal base panel and corners. A new cushion was introduced incorporating its own millboard base and, in general, the appearance now closely followed the back seat. This basic seat cushion was unchanged thereafter in production.

341500 Bottom edge of front mudguard changed behind bumper bar apron to lengthen stiffened turn-down and add strength to anchorage point for the diagonal pressed stay.

341700 Roof light changed from ornamental chrome and cut-glass style to a more modern oblong plastic lens which was more functional at the price of cheaper appearance. This occurred at six-light body number 25/1/1501, the four-light body number was not recorded.

342600 Carpet colour changed from standardized fawn/camel colour to match exactly the interior leather work in all cases except where white or ivory leather was used; in these few cases the carpet usually matched the seat piping which was usually colour coordinated to the car's paintwork.

343751 Mark 2 chassis (and model) introduced with many detailed changes and improvements including: **(a)** Rubber stoneguards to front of rear spats (many Mark 1 cars when used in stony situations have subsequently had this modification done). (**b**) New door base rubber seals with revised position for attachment channel. (**c**) Rubber seals introduced to base of centre pillar and at front mudguard/door reveal bottom. (**d**) Scuttle side trims now in carpet instead of cream millboard. (**e**) Stiffening under front seat runners introduced, and new widened spacer pieces, (carpet covered in place of vinyl). This ensured that a 20 stone occupant descending on the seat without thought would not bend the floor! (**f**) Tail lights now with red glass in lieu of white/opalescent fluted glass covers. (**g**) Reverse lights now wired to light assembly above number plate, winking turn indicators standardized for all deliveries. (**h**) Automatic cars have 'Sapphire Automatic' in a script badge added to the centre of the bootlid. (**i**) Modified instrument panel introduced with larger ultraviolet-lit instruments. Ammeter now incorporated in minor instrument cluster and four new warning lights added just above the steering column.

344500 Radio aperture enlarged to accommodate a broad spectrum of proprietary radios made to a standardized size. This modification was not intoduced exclusively at a certain point in the production run; quite a number of cars from about chassis 344100 had the larger aperture prior to its universal adoption.

345001 Rear tail lights again changed to have a red reflex plastic lens with reflector incorporated; many earlier cars have been retrospectively so fitted as the red glass lens hid the winking turn light too much and many licencing authorities insisted on upgrading.

346001 Rear ashtray surround simplified.

346501 Power steering control quadrant (if fitted) modified to be similar to the choke control quadrant surround, half-moon quadrant cover abandoned. Control quadrant now mounted within instrument panel rather than in bottom edge.

346501 Fine lining (coach lining) on wheels deleted.

346501 Leather handle/strap added to tool drawer end for easier use.

347001 Rear ashtray surround entirely deleted as on last of Whitleys.

347250 (Sept 1957) Major modification to limousine body work: wheelarches changed to minimum wheel clearance, thus giving maximum rear seat width, jump seat mountings changed to give more leg room.

347297 Saloon rear side armrests cut back to provide easy ingress and egress; these were even more severely cut back than the later treatment used on the Star Sapphire.

347297 Sphinx mascot changed to a brass pressing in lieu of the alloy casting. These later sphinxs had a sloping rear end instead of a vertical cut-off, so the central chrome bonnet strip was also modified to eliminate a visible joint between it and the mascot when viewed from the driving position – a great improvement carried out rather too late in the production run.

347307 The standard Mark 2 speedometer dial changed, with calibrations now reading on the even rather than the odd numbers. There was an extended line added to the 30mph position.

Limousine

During 1955 a limousine was launched on a special stretched Sapphire chassis, the wheelbase having been increased to 11ft 1in from the normal 9ft 6in. The extra space thus gained was entirely devoted to the rear passenger area. The long chassis enabled the factory to produce an elegant and stately formal car. Although it appeared to be an enlarged standard saloon, most panels were different. The only common panels were the bonnet, bootlid, radiator grille bars, front bumper apron and bumper bars. All other panels and the main body shell are special to the limousine. Like most formal limousines the Sapphire had a higher roof line to enable easy

1955 Sapphire 346 long-wheelbase chassis C345769 with the seventh limousine body to be built, number 25/4/0007, retained by the factory as a demonstrator. Though it looked at a quick glance just like an enlarged standard saloon, most aspects of the limousine design were subtly reworked so that there were in fact very few common panels.

Rear three-quarter view of the limousine. A wheelbase 19in longer than that of the saloon allowed ample space for passenger accommodation.

ingress and egress from the rear seat and enough headroom for passengers using the occasional seats. In an effort to ensure that the car did not look too top heavy, all the lower panels too were increased about two inches in height to provide the necessary aesthetic balance, and two slightly different roof lines were used.

The body, although mostly of steel construction, had a massive wooden central cross structure that carried the sliding glass division. The front seat frame and its encased ends became the front door hanging posts. The woodwork was very strong but subject to dry rot in humid conditions. The whole of this structural woodwork division was beautifully covered in leather or cloth trim and polished woodwork, with the door post ends capped in panel steel. There was also a small amount of structural woodwork for the rear door posts and around the rear quarter windows.

The body otherwise closely followed the structural design and production methods of the saloon. There were many areas that were different to the saloon including a revised boot floor to accommodate the wider spare tyre, a rear bumper apron not standard on the saloons, an elaborate rear floor pan with recessed areas for jump seat occupants' feet, large leather door check straps and a rear

Another view of the factory limousine demonstrator, an imposing and elegant formal carriage, its style nicely balanced between traditional and modern.

114

compartment entry step with the cutaway part attached to the door to complete the floor once closed. But the real changes were in the level of amenity and appointment. The rear compartment was serviced by an elaborate fresh-air heater that took air from beside the radiator, ducted it to a large heat exchanger and fan located under the front seat and then redirected the hot air out through special ducts on either side of the division. The rear heaters were entirely separate from the front heaters and controlled at a panel situated in the lefthand rear side armrest.

A separate rear clock was located above the glass division, centrally mounted. Twin roof lights for the rear passengers and a central roof light on the division provided interior illumination, the rear lights having both automatic control and manual override.

Inside the rear compartment of a standard 346 limousine with leather trim in place of the West of England cloth which was often specified. Note how the cutout step is filled when the door is closed to provide a level floor.

One of the rare limousines to be finished by the factory in two-tone paintwork. This car has the standard West of England cloth trim and rear seat over-cushions. 'To the Palace, James.'

There were twin panic straps for rear occupants, a thick mohair overcarpet rug for the rear compartment, a special storage compartment under the driver's seat, plaited rope door pulls fitted to rear doors, and a rear window blind with the chauffeur regulating its use by a slide control above the driver's door.

The limousine interiors were mostly fitted out with leather trim for the front seat and West of England cloth for the rear seats, with the balance of the trim in the compartments matching. However, cars could be ordered with full leather trim as were the 15 that were delivered to the Australian Government VIP fleet.

Full refrigerated air conditioning was installed in some cars, operated from a rear mounted plant, with ducted cold air supply vents above the door openings. Most, if not all, cars, so fitted were delivered to the Middle East. There were also an assortment of special extras available for ceremonial use including the traditional flag pole which was mounted behind the mascot, the mast of which could be removed and replaced with a screwed-in plug.

A considerable number of these limousines had modifications to suit the customer's special needs. There was a Swiss customer who wanted a car with a very high roof line while another wanted a toilet and one, believe it or not, wanted leopard skin trim. The factory accommodated all these requests within their flexible organisation.

The 'standard issue' formal limousine came with black paintwork, black leather trim in the front compartment and fawn West of England cloth in the rear compartment. The alternative colours for paintwork offered from the list were Elephant Grey, Pearl Grey,

116

Silver Grey, Corinthian Green, Langham Grey and Dark Blue, but many cars were delivered with other colours chosen by the customer. Interior colours in leather were red, brown, beige, green and blue.

All appointments were of the highest quality and the level of overall finish made the limousine a top class luxury vehicle. During September 1957 the limousine body underwent a series of minor changes that improved the overall space and comfort without altering the exterior dimensions. The body width between the rear seat side arm rests was increased by an extra 2½in to 50in, the knee

Full leather trim in the rear of 1956 limousine, chassis C346495, originally one of 14 in the Australian government VIP fleet, now owned by K. Bartenstein.

Driving compartment of a 1956 limousine with synchromesh gearbox. Quarter lights differ in shape from those of the saloon.

Pictures from 1957 of a limousine to special order for a desert climate. Intake vents at the rear of the turret are evidence of an extra-large air conditioning plant installed in the boot, and its associated condenser rather than mere extravagance of styling probably explains the flamboyant grille. This car has often been thought to have been the one supplied to the Shah of Persia but the loss of records relating chassis numbers to photographs makes it impossible to verify this identity with total certainty.

room between the rear seat and the backs of the jump seats when in use was increased from 26½in to 29½in, while the knee room for the jump seat passengers was increased by 1½in to 25in. These changes occurred from body number 25-4-0259, or about two-thirds of the way through the limousine's production run.

The first limousine chassis produced was number 345653 and their issue continued intermingled with standard-length units until chassis number 347646, the discontinuation of the standard chassis length. The production of limousines actually continued well into 1959 as the Star Sapphire came out in saloon form only first and was not followed with the companion limousine until 1960. The non-availability of Star limousines during 1959 ensured the continuity of 346 limousine production well past the cut-off date for the 346 saloon. There is little doubt that the Sapphire limousine was a successful vehicle; it went almost as fast as the saloon and handled and rode at least as well. For such a limited and formal market, the production of 381 units was no mean achievement.

118

Oil company pick-up

During the period 1955/6 the Armstrong Siddeley Motors marketing division were exploring new markets. Their contact with the oil companies in the Middle East led them to believe that there was a market for a heavy duty, open light truck. To meet a perceived demand initially estimated at 250 units, the factory produced a pick-up truck built on the standard 346 chassis. The concept was to produce a very rugged, high ground clearance vehicle, with all but the load bed and the back of the cabin using standard 346 components, but with a significantly reduced level of body finish.

The specification called for a total absence of woodwork, both in the body structure and for ornamentation. The appointments were to be adequate but sparse and the gearbox was to be the normal synchromesh issue, chosen as the cheapest of the three

transmissions. All chrome plating was deleted with everything sprayed normal body colour. The headlights were changed to the cheap sealed beam type, and so on.

The prevailing understanding of this oil company market was that so little care was taken of machinery that when it broke down, or ran out of oil or petrol, nobody bothered to repair it, but just pushed it into the nearest wadi and left it to rot. Believing this to be true, Armstrong Siddeley Motors had hopes of reasonable volume sales. They even produced an austerity version of the 346 saloon for this market and sold a few.

However, their expectations were not met. There was an initial batch run of 41 pick-up trucks, then a further four were built, of which only three were exported, with the last or 45th remaining with the factory as a runaround. This vehicle still exists and at the time of writing is owned by Mr J.V. Burns in London. The fate of the other

Attracted by the possibility of a lucrative market among the oil companies in the Middle East, Armstrong Siddeley embarked on the production of this pick-up based on the standard length Sapphire 346 chassis. Mechanical components and the front-end body panels were mostly standard, uprated where necessary for ruggedness and increased ground clearance. Despite the number plate fitted for this factory photograph, these vehicles were built during 1956 and 1957.

Three more views of the oil company pick-up, showing clearly the saloon-based front bodywork and the spartan, strictly utility level of trim and appointments. Unfortunately the project failed to take off commercially, and production ceased after only 45 examples.

44 remains a mystery – one can only hope that perhaps a handful survive today.

The production problems of lack of demand were further compounded by the fact that, within the 45-unit production run, there were many minor specification variations to suit customers, such as a considerable variety of wheel and tyre sizes. The whole exercise, while historically interesting, is hardly likely to have been profitable. These pick-up trucks would have been built in the latter part of 1956 and into early 1957, all being Mark 2 specifications. Chassis numbers are listed in Appendix 13.

On the road
At the risk of appearing to be a little biased, I feel that the Sapphire is one of the most outstanding cars of the 1950s. Among its contemporaries only a handful of exotic supercars offered a better all round performance and serviceability package. The particular virtues it offered were fatigue-free long distance travel, excellent forward vision for all passengers, a modest thirst, ease of service, good ground clearance and long suspension travel, a large boot space, superb appearance and, to the discerning driver, wonderful handling.

For this combination of reasons the Sapphire found its way not only to what we might now call the executive purchaser, the customer its manufacturers might reasonably be supposed to have had in mind, but to the person that wanted a high quality car for hard commercial work and reliability in rough conditions. In Australia about a third of all new sales were to the outback, where, as already mentioned, road conditions were far beyond the car's design criteria. Yet they fared very well and many can be found scattered throughout Australia, rather than clustered in capital cities like most other 'quality' cars, and many are still working very hard for their owners.

The Sapphire is a relatively large car yet handles crisply: it has mild understeering characteristics and becomes neutral when power is applied in a corner. It corners very flat and yet rides softly. Its behaviour on gravel and dirt roads is very similar to the behaviour on tarmacadam, making high speed use in these conditions still practical. In the wet the car also handles in an exemplary manner, assuming you have good tyres. Thus it is an exceptional all round highway and byway car.

The engine was outstanding at the time of introduction; by today's standards, some 30 years later, it equates to a mundane mass-produced car in road performance. The Sapphire will accelerate from rest to 50mph in just over seven seconds if it is fitted with twin carburettors and a preselective gearbox, still an acceptable figure. On the road the Sapphire driver generally finds himself wanting to overtake most other traffic, for the car just lopes along in the mid 80s and will comfortably travel all day into the middle to higher 90s. A well maintained and fully run-in car will just exceed 100mph and some have been timed at close to 110mph. Driven flat out the car still handles beautifully.

The other side of the Sapphire's performance is its slow running high torque output at low engine speeds. This gives great flexibility for town and traffic use. Such flexibility can be no better demonstrated than with a top gear start on a level road: the car will gently glide away without snatch or judder – this, of course, can only

Very special equipment fitted to the 1954 Sapphire, registration number RAR 700, which Mike Couper drove in the Monte Carlo Rally: headlamp wipers, long before they became common production items, and an extendible lamp mounting which, whatever the theory behind it, probably had more to do with winning the concours and equipment awards which were then still a feature of the event than it did with any practical purpose.

be demonstrated in preselective and synchromesh gearbox cars!

Sapphire facts

The first preselective Sapphire (having gearbox number PS340002) was chassis 340001.

The last preselective Sapphire (having gearbox number PS34408 was chassis 347590.

The first synchromesh Sapphire (having gearbox number SAS5) was chassis 340021.

The last synchromesh Sapphire (having gearbox number SAS2694) was chassis 347697.

The first (production) automatic Sapphire (having gearbox number C23) was chassis 343823.

The last (production) automatic Sapphire saloon (having gearbox number CZ1932) was chassis 347639.

The last automatic Sapphire limousine (having gearbox number CZ2056) was chassis 347695.

The first six-light saloon body (number 25/1/0001) was on chassis 340004.

The last six-light saloon body (number 25/1/6870) was on chassis 347646.

The first four-light saloon body (number 25/2/0001) was on chassis 340001.

The last four-light saloon body to be made (number 25/2/0381) was on chassis 347301.

The last four-light saloon body to be fitted (number 25/2/0377) was on chassis 347307.

The first limousine body (number 25/4/0001) was on chassis 345653. The last limousine body (number 25/4/0381) was on chassis 347697.

Limousine body 25/4/0352 was built without division on chassis 347670.

Chassis 346967 had four-light body 25/4/0366 (which was built with semaphore indicators in lieu of winkers).

Chassis 341450 had 'hot' engine S/EX/2 (Registration number ORW 429).

Mk 1 chassis numbered 342987, 343288, 343289, 343444, 343563, 343605, 343681, and 343708 were all converted to full Mark 2 specifications by the factory prior to sale.

Mk 1 chassis numbered 343639 and 343692 were converted by the experimental department to automatic Mk 2 specifications.

Chassis supplied to various outside coachbuilders were numbered 345896, 346510, 347063, 347265, 347295, 347296, 347361, 347363, 347364, 347365, 347366, 347367, 346368, 3473469, 347370, 34744.

There were only 31 Mark 2 Sapphires with four-light bodies.

Preselective gearbox number sequence in production cars was PS340002 to PS344008.

Automatic gearbox numbering in production cars was CZ5 to CZ2056 (these numbers not quite sequential), balance were probably fitted to Bentley and Rolls-Royce cars of the same production period excepting two fitted on Mk 1 Sapphire chassis by Armstrong Siddeley Motors.

Synchromesh gearbox numbers have one of two letter prefixes followed by four digits. The prefixes are 'SAS' and 'SASL' but the difference between them is not recorded nor by physical inspection can it be determined. The fourth prefix letter does not indicate lefthand drive. These numbering sequences are also not fully sequential: the earliest recorded number on a production car was SAS 1 and the last used SAS 2794. The SASL series were used from quite early in the Mark 1 series and were scattered throughout the earlier production cars, among the first series with the other prefix.

As not every gearbox produced or bought-in was used in production, some being experimental or sold for spares – naturally there would have been a few warranty claims as well – it is not possible to establish accurately how many of each were actually fitted to cars built. However, the following estimate would be a realistic close approximation: preselective, 4000; synchromesh, 1650; automatic, 2050.

Preselective gearbox number 1 (PS340001) was fitted to experimental 340 Sapphire chassis EXPR/340/11 while the first synchromesh gearbox SAS 1 was not used until the 60th production chassis was built (chassis 340060).

Mystery car: little is known about the 346 limousine in this factory photograph. The chrome strip on the bootlid, early pattern tail lights, semaphore turn indicators and saloon hubcaps all suggest that it is a 1953 model, hence predating the launch of the limousine in production form. The rear corners of the roof panel are markedly more rounded than those of the later series-built cars. It may well be that this is the fifth of the 'Vincent' limousines, chassis EXLC/340/5, but available records do not confirm the registration number.

Vincent limousines

The factory records refer to a group of Mark 1 chassis entitled 'Vincent' limousines: the data surrounding these cars is shrouded in mystery and none seem to have survived. All were used by Armstrong Siddeley Motors or Hawker Siddeley group executives, all had experimental chassis, one had an experimental engine, and all had an L prefix to a typical Armstrong Siddeley Sapphire body number. All have early engine numbers but are far from sequential. Delivery dates for four of the five cars differ by up to almost a year. One may perhaps assume that the L in the chassis number sequence denotes long chassis, while EX is customary for any experimental items. I list the recorded data on these cars in Appendix 14 and hope some reader in the future can enlighten me further, and perhaps let me have authenticated photographs or information, should any car still exist. I suspect that in accordance with company policy on experimental cars, all were broken up by Armstrong Siddeley Motors at the end of their useful life.

4

Promise unfulfilled

The 234 and 236 Sapphires, 1956 to 1958
With the Sapphire model successfully established, by 1953/54 the factory were free to design and tool up for a smaller model intended to be a genuine replacement for the now discontinued 16/18hp range. The larger Sapphire had carved its own market share very well, but was not in all cases satisfying the traditional medium sized car purchaser who had historically been a large proportion of the Armstrong Siddeley market since the mid 1920s. It was this fact, coupled with the already evident beginning of a trend in public opinion towards smaller cars, which led the factory to decide to introduce a new smaller range, not as a replacement for the successful Sapphire, but as a supplementary model programme. This was exactly the same path chosen by Jaguar in a similar period of time; they too introduced new smaller models, the 2.4 and 3.4-litre Mk 1 saloons, which were to become the market-place competition for the new Armstrong Siddeley cars.

For the Motor Show in 1955, then, the public were surprised to see two new Sapphire models on the Armstrong Siddeley stand, in company with the larger Sapphire, making the line up. The new models were a radical departure from the traditional Armstrong Siddeley appearance, and were possibly too advanced in their style for what was still a fairly conservative era. This no doubt did not suit a great number of Armstrong Siddeley customers who were mostly traditional in their taste.

These two new cars were named after the bigger Sapphire hoping to ride on the great success of their bigger brother. To differentiate, the factory chose the prefix numbers 234 and 236 before the word Sapphire to designate each model, the first two digits indicating 2.3 litres in engine capacity while the last digit denoted the number of cylinders (the same procedure being adopted for the larger car which thus became the 346 Sapphire).

In my view this name was an unwise decision as the new cars looked entirely different and this caused the bulk of the public to become confused, one reason for the sales expectations for the models never being achieved. These newcomers should been given totally new names: instead, they got the rather derogatory tag 'baby Sapphires' and soon became known by their model number – 234 or 236 – rather than by name as the public had already related to the big and beautiful Sapphire as being the only rightful owner of the title.

The 234 and 236 models were an outstanding design but, like so many other well engineered cars over the decades, were not a commercial success. The writer can well remember visiting the regional executive manager for Hawker Siddeley in Australia, back in 1960: he said that he had a 236, which he liked very much, but described the model series as 'the company's most successful mistake'. In these words he said it all. The total production of only 1,406 over a three-year period illustrates this point. Contemporary writers on motoring matters suggest the highly successful smaller Jaguars were the cause of the poor market performance of the 234 and 236 Sapphires. This, while true in part, is not the main reason

Factory photograph from 1955 of one of the first 236 Sapphires built. The styling was to prove perhaps the most controversial aspect of the model, many people feeling that Armstrong Siddeley's attempt to produce a thoroughly up-to-date shape was not entirely successful.

1955 Sapphire 236, chassis C230003, retained by the factory as a demonstrator. Whatever the arguments over the aesthetics of the body, in practical terms it worked very well, providing good visibility for all the occupants and generating very little wind noise at speed.

for the low production as many dealers' orders were cancelled due to the inability of the factory to supply the required volumes. Ironically, there is little doubt that these new smaller Sapphires focussed renewed attention on their bigger brother whose sales boomed.

At approximately the same time as the 234 and 236 were launched, the parent company became even more heavily involved in defence and aircraft manufacture and decided to concentrate resources in these other more lucrative areas as profit was assured. So the 234/236 series were batch run in the 346 assembly area and never really carved out their own manufacturing niche. Staff at the now defunct Buckle Motors Ltd in Sydney told me that they had orders for 78 of these cars, most of which were presold, yet the Armstrong Siddeley factory never issued a single 234/236 to them for sale. In fact Australia only received four cars through the dealer network, three 236s and one 234, and there were two other private importations.

Coming now to the cars themselves as opposed to the historical circumstances, facts and myths surrounding them, I feel it was a clear case of the right cars launched at the wrong moment. In appearance, these cars seemed to many people to be either ugly or uninteresting – they had only the radiator grille left to relate to perceived ideas of what an Armstrong Siddeley should look like. The body was of the full width concept with no intrusion even for rear wheelarches, while the chassis followed closely the lines of a scaled down 346 Sapphire. The engine was either an upgraded version of the 18hp Whitley-style motor for the 236 or two-thirds of a 346 Sapphire motor for the 234. The higher performance model was the four-cylinder 234 and this further confused the public, being entirely contrary to motoring tradition.

126

The body shape was so engineered, drawing on aircraft principles, that you could turn the engine off at 90mph and find yourself in an almost entirely noise-free environment, wind noise being almost eliminated. These cars were free of faults at release, with only minor modifications needed during the production run. The only problem was rust where they were exposed to salty conditions, as the sheet steel was kept thinner than previous models to ensure weight reduction and fuel economy. They only weighed about 27cwt and when fitted with an overdrive could achieve close to 30 miles per gallon on a trip, which was good when you consider the massively strong chassis that was provided.

Standard equipment was a truly delightful all-synchromesh four-speed sports gearbox of Armstrong Siddeley design and manufacture. The 236 models were frequently fitted with the Manumatic clutch, providing two-pedal motoring, and both the 234 and the 236 were optionally available with the renowned Laycock de Normanville overdrive. An automatic was never offered nor apparently was the traditional preselective, yet we do know of at least one 236 with a factory fitted preselective gearbox (chassis 230276). This car has the 16/18hp preselective gearbox and all details concerning the production and fitment of the gearbox are available in spare parts records. Thus it is highly likely that there may have been a few others. The 234 could also have been had with a special competition engine and clutch but again how many were built is not known; none having this level of tune and equipment have come to light in recent years. Likewise wire wheels as an extra were available, being offered to purchasers for either four or six-cylinder cars, but the choice was only taken by 234 buyers. All other extras and options were of the more cosmetic nature such as radio, wheel trims for disc wheels and so on.

127

1958 Sapphire 234 when brand new, fitted with optional chrome plated wire wheels complete with knock-off hubs.

Although this model was dubbed the 'baby Sapphire' by the public, its small size was only relative to the 346 Sapphire which was quite a large car. The 234/236 was a full and very commodious five-seater car, having plenty of body width and most generous leg and head room, making it one car that really suited a tall person. The boot space was adequate rather than generous. The overall width was 5ft 8in and the overall length 15ft, making it a full medium sized car, yet it was compact and manoeuvrable in traffic. As public taste has changed, and competitors' cars have become more modern, the 234/236 has become more accepted and better appreciated. Its success as a long life, driver's car has been realized and its freedom from developing body faults and rattles makes a high mileage example still a delight to drive.

The 234 model chassis numbers are 4230003, and 4230007 to 4230803 plus 8 cars made using the 236 chassis number sequence, these being 230045, 230061, 230065, 230103, 230105, 230109, together with the two original factory demonstrators F230004 (SDU

1957 Sapphire 234, chassis C4230454, fitted with over-drive, fog lights, mirrors and stone guards, all factory extras. This beautifully preserved car, owned by Mrs. P. Elliott, may well be the best example in the world.

128

666) and F230005 (RVC 907). In most, if not all cases, these 236 series numbers were prefixed with the letter F for 'Four', but the factory decided to use the figure 4 once production commenced in earnest. The one odd exception was 4230003 (RVC 905), the Coventry demonstrator which had the original 4 prefix yet came out of the 236 chassis number run. Thus total production was 806 of which there were 803 standard saloons plus one bodied by Michelotti, one utility built out of a modified standard body by the Armstrong Siddeley experimental department, plus an attractive in-house produced sports car, pictures of which seem to be lost. 236 model chassis numbers are 230001 to 230609 less eight chassis built as 234s out of this production run. Thus total production was 601.

These figures tally with the body build of 1,404 standard saloon bodies, of which 1,403 were used without alteration. The overall production of both types was 1,406. The 234 was built from April 1956 until October 1958, and the 236 from January 1956 until June 1957. Sales, of course, continued well past the last production dates.

Ease of entry and egress for both front and rear passengers was a feature of the 234/236 design. This was the first Armstrong Siddeley to have front-hinged front doors.

The chassis frame

The 234/236 chassis was built along very similar lines to that of the 346 Sapphire, its significant differences being a simpler, less bulky central cruciform section, a welded-in front crossmember designed to give more suspension travel and minimize chassis flex, and different jacking points as well as its generally smaller size. It gave the smaller Sapphires a wheelbase of 111in which was only 3in shorter than that of the 346, but the overall design was such that these cars, when completed, were 1ft 1in shorter than the standard 346 and 3½in narrower overall, though the passenger space was actually larger. These chassis frames were even stiffer than the earlier version and were structurally totally trouble free in service. It is indeed a pity that only one chassis was bodied by an outside coachbuilding company, as the overall engineering of the completed and assembled chassis was so successful.

The suspension and steering

The front suspension was built along similar lines to the 346 Sapphire but featured different top wishbones, heavily curved, which, with the heightened crossmember, gave the suspension greater travel. The pivot points on the front suspension were all

The chassis of the 234/236 Sapphire. This example is fitted with a 236 engine, manual gearbox and Laycock de Normanville overdrive. The design evolved from that of the earlier Sapphire, the cruciform centre section giving way to this cross-braced twin-rail layout.

mounted in Metalastik rubber/steel bushes, the top inner pivot being totally different to the threaded one in the 346. Most of the other suspension components were actually the same as the Mark 2 Sapphire excepting spring rates which of course were adjusted for a lighter car.

The rear suspension was also similar to the 346 but marginally lighter in construction. The leaf springs were of the semi-elliptic type but sat nearly flat when mounted and loaded. The body roll was controlled with front and rear anti-roll bars, again mounted in rubber.

The steering was by a Burman F-type steering box which featured a variable ratio and the recirculating ball type drive. The steering column in this case was not adjustable and the steering wheel was a smaller version of the 346 wheel and identical to the 18hp utility models. Overall the suspension system worked particularly well, giving the car a flat and smooth ride with minimal pitch or unwanted movement. Whilst the steering and handling characteristics were similar to those of their bigger brother, these cars had a more taut and sports car like feel.

The 234/236 models were mostly fitted with four Girling tubular shock absorbers for general issue. However, the Armstrong brand heavy duty shock absorbers were available to order for cars being

130

Details of the rear end of the 234/236 chassis and rear suspension, including angled telescopic shock absorbers and curved anti-roll bar.

used in rough terrain. A couple of examples had the Teleflow adjustable rear shock absorbers fitted, again as a special order. The front shock absorbers were mounted concentrically within the coil springs, while the rear ones were mounted leaning in at about a 60-degree angle, now common practice for many manufacturers, but not so common at that time.

Shock absorber technology had advanced very significantly in the ten years since the first 16hp car was built and the 234/236 equipment represented the state of the art at that time and the start of the current era of design. Some owners today are fitting their 234/236 cars with Koni gas shock absorbers and report a further significant improvement in ride and handling, making the cars so equipped right up to modern standards.

The brakes

The 234/236 braking system is a smaller copy of the Mark 2 Sapphire system, with the boosted trailing-shoe drum layout that Girling had perfected. In this case the drums were of 11in diameter and $2\frac{1}{4}$in wide, identical to the Mark 1 Sapphire 346 drums. The whole system was initially boosted by a Clayton Dewandre booster, which at body number 181201 (after the first 1,200 cars were built) was changed to a Girling Mark 2 booster of a more advanced design. The handbrake was a centrally mounted lever similar to many sports cars and operated the rear brakes by cable. This braking system was more than adequate for the high performance of the 234 and with the generous drum width and diameter provided adequate cooling and thus was capable of being used safely for repeated high speed stops. The performance of this system probably represents the pinnacle of drum brake design. Disc brakes were at the time only just being used in racing cars and were under evaluation by Armstrong Siddeley motors. An owner of a 234/236 can rest in the knowledge that his/her car will be well able to meet the demands of modern highway and traffic conditions.

The engines

These models had two entirely different engines, both however of 2.3-litre capacity and both having their origins in previous models. The 234 engine, a new four-cylinder unit, was broadly speaking two-thirds of a 346 Sapphire engine hotted up to give a similar bhp output. To achieve this power the engine incorporated much that was to become standard issue in the Star Sapphire engine. There were new valves, main bearings, con rod bearings, crankshaft steel type, higher crown pistons and so on. The 234 engine gave 120bhp in standard twin SU carburettor form, only 5bhp less than a standard

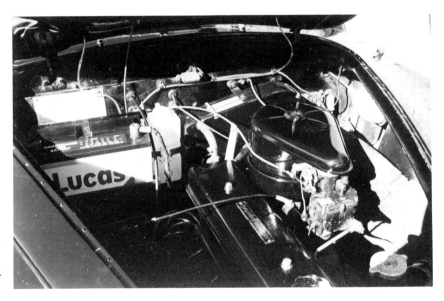

236 engine compartment: this is chassis C230445, a car equipped with a conventional clutch and hence lacking the extra controls of the Manumatic system.

single carburettor 346 Sapphire engine. This engine is a willing performer, being very robust, and is felt by many, including the designer, to be the best of all the Sapphire engines. Its numbering series begins E234 plus four other digits.

The 236 engine was basically a reworked late 18hp engine with significant changes to pistons, wet liners, cylinder head, valves, engine block, sump, oil filter, water pump mountings and so on, producing virtually a new engine. This engine gave an output of 85bhp against the 75 for the last of the 18hp or Whitley engines. There were two most signficant changes as far as the operation of the engine was concerned, one being that the sealing ring grooves were now cut into the cylinder liners instead of the block, thus stiffening up the block and also making it easier to clean up when new liners were to be fitted. The other significant change was the introduction of the paper element oil filter which was standardized for 234, 346 and this engine. These engines last far better than the 16/18hp series, mainly because of better filtration.

132

In appearance, the 236 engine is so like the 18hp engine, that, at first glance, you can easily be mistaken. The gasket set is exactly the same for both excepting the oil filter base gasket and the water pump base gasket. The 236 engine number begins E236 and has four other digits while, of course, a 16hp engine number begins E16 and an 18hp engine number begins E18.

When the factory decided to introduce the 234/236 models, they must have perceived their market as being spread in a way towards each end of the car buying spectrum, for the 234 was really a very sporty car, while the 236 may be described as adequate in performance but having a somewhat staid, 'Aunty' image. The 234 would exceed 100mph if overdrive were fitted, while the 236 had a top speed generally in the mid 80s and could only just scrape over the 90mph mark if overdrive were fitted and long open roads were available. It was the way these speeds were delivered that made the cars so different to drive.

It is interesting to view the production and sales statistics as they go a long way to telling the story. Almost all the 'baby' Sapphire production for 1956 was the 236 version with only a handful of 234s actually built. Most 236s were fitted with the Manumatic version of the synchromesh gearbox. This pattern particularly applies to the first 500 or about 80% of production, in which there were very few 236s built with the conventional clutch and overdrive except for a handful of export orders: at about chassis 230500 the pattern changed and some began to have overdrive. This pattern tends to confirm the observation of the type of customer that the 236 model attracted. This engine variant was terminated in 1957 as, by that time, the 234 had become accepted.

Coming now to the 234, the public, at that time, saw four-cylinder engines as down market low-performance derivatives, illustrated for example by the distinction in the Vauxhall range between Wyvern and Velox, and I believe there was quite a lot of buyer resistance at first. Thus for most of 1956 the 234s were largely forgotten by the public. However, gradually the message got around that the 234 was a real 'goer' and very different from the rather sober 236. So by early in 1957 the emphasis had started to change and by mid 1957 the 234 became the only car to buy and continued in production until late 1958. Many 234s were fitted with the optional overdrive, and the Manumatic clutch was not available. To complete the sports car image many were fitted with wire wheels.

Both engine derivatives are entirely satisfactory, it just becomes a matter of choice and requirement. However, the current trend, in the present secondhand market, is such that the 234 brings far higher prices than the equivalent 236. Both engines are very long life units and provided they are serviced and used properly; they can still be in untouched excellent condition at 100,000 miles. One 236 engine (E2360459) in Australia is credited with over three hundred thousand miles of use and has had only one major overhaul during its life and that, in mileage terms, is only recently.

The main distinguishing features of the 234 engine compared to the 346 engine, other than being a four-cylinder unit, are: pistons have higher dome for a 7.5:1 compression ratio; valves bigger, inlet tulip shape as fitted to the Star engine; heavy duty connecting rods as on the Star engine; twin SU HD6 carburettors; special gas flow exhaust manifolds; large capacity sump spread for oil cooling; distributor drive with take-off for revolution counter; main and big-end bearings heavy duty as on the Star; and twin bobbin type front engine mounts.

The 236 engine, compared to the last series 18hp engine, had: higher compression ratio (7:5:1); new pistons; bigger inlet valves; new cylinder liners with three O-ring sealing grooves; changed camshaft profiles; smaller capacity oil sump; new oil filter (same as 346 Sapphire); modified rocker cover; upgraded main and big-end bearings; new design for water pump; modified cylinder head; modified cylinder block; solid rather than hydraulic tappets (as on last of 18hp engines); and bobbin type front engine mounts.

The 234/236 models had a single silencer exhaust system which was hung in figure-8 brackets. The silencers were different between the 234 and the 236, each type being tuned to the specific characteristics of the engine as the requirements were significantly different. These silencers are not used on any other Armstrong Siddeley model.

The 234/236 had rather squat and relatively wide brass and copper radiators to cope with the low frontal design of the body. They were still of the vertical flow type and varied from 234 to 236, as the heat dissipation requirements were markedly different. These radiators were bottom mounted and unlike on any previous Armstrong Siddeley slid into their mounting cradle from beneath the front of the car. They were secured by two simple rubber insulated fixings at the sides and had two padded bottom mounting bolts.

Early in the life of the 234 it was found that the original four rows of radiator tubes were inadequate for hot climate operations and a five-row radiator together with a fan cowl was introduced. Many cars that were issued with the four-row radiator were recalled and had the new radiator and cowl fitted; at the same time a new fan was installed, of a seven-bladed type in lieu of the more normal five-blade type, increasing the air flow capacity. The fan was mounted on the block (unlike the 346) beneath the water pump. All export 234s from March 1957 manufacture had these modifications as standard issue. These cooling systems were adequate rather than overdesigned and worked well so long as they were not allowed to become clogged by the unwise use of inappropriate water.

To fill these radiators there was a rightangle filler neck and extension located at the front edge of the engine bay opening. It was quite easy to fill but the filler neck arrangement prevented the owner from being able to check the water level visually, the radiator being mounted well forward of the bonnet edge.

The transmission
The 234 and the non-Manumatic 236s were fitted with a standard conventional Borg and Beck clutch which was operated hydraulically. The 234 clutch was type 9A6G while the 236s were fitted with a similar but no doubt lighter duty clutch, type 9AG-G. Alternative to this was the Manumatic or pedaless clutch which was

only available on the 236 cars. This was quite an elaborate arrangement which, while in itself satisfactory, was only popular for a short period. Much of this lack of popularity probably stemmed from problems in service with untrained personnel and a general public apprehension of the system. Soon, the Manumatic had a bad reputation and other manufacturers, as well as Armstrong Siddeley, quickly deleted the option. However, those that were correctly serviced have stood the test of time over 30 years and still work well, having proven their success in defiance of the critics.

The Manumatic clutch system enables the driver to pull up or take off without needing to use a conventional clutch, in much the same way as with an automatic gearbox. Housed in the gearlever knob is a micro switch which activates the clutch mechanism during up or down gear changes. To achieve such simplicity of use it required a servo to operate the clutch, a control unit consisting of two solenoids and various valves and levers, a linkage to the carburettor to control the engine function, and the attendant electrical wiring and hydraulic couplings.

To drive the Manumatic 236 was a cross between driving a manual car and a fully automatic car – you had a conventional gearlever and no sign of a clutch! When you wished to take off from rest all you did was push the gearlever into first or reverse and then pull away just by pressing the accelerator. Gear changes were accomplished simply by moving the lever. When you wished to stop, you just depressed the brake. The Manumatic clutch and its systems was made by Automotive Products of Leamington Spa. Approximately 450 of the 601 236s were so equipped: the greater proportion of standard-clutch 236s commenced after chassis number 230461.

Interestingly, a system which achieved similar results in a slightly different way was offered in more recent times as an option by, among others, Fiat, Volkswagen and Porsche, the latter company coining the name 'Sportomatic' for their version, and it proved to have only a slightly longer spell of popularity.

The only other alternative which was used for both the 234 and 236 was the preselective gearbox. This version is shrouded in mystery, for the factory spares schedules and drawings – as opposed to dealer spare parts lists – show both models as having been made with preselective gears at some stage, but how many were so produced is unknown and only one 236 is known to survive. From an inspection of the parts manufacturing list the indication is that the 236 used the 18hp model's Newton clutch and gearbox while the 234 used the 346 Sapphire type Newton clutch and gearbox. As far as the general public were aware the 234 and 236 cars were all fitted with an upgraded and substantially revised version of the 16/18hp gearbox. This gearbox was of Armstrong Siddeley production and is one of the most delightful of all sports type manual gearboxes that I have ever used (including the 1980s Japanese gearboxes): it gives no indication of its early heritage and with its stubby gearshift lever it was far better to use than most other gearboxes of its era.

The gearlever was centrally mounted with semi-remote control. It controlled an all synchromesh four-speed gearbox with inertia-lock synchronizing cones. This enabled very fast gear changes – it seemed impossible ever to beat the synchromesh action if the gearbox were in good order. The central lever was spring biased in two directions, reverse was protected with quite a heavy spring, while another lighter spring pushed the lever away from the third/fourth plane to centralize it in the gate. Once you got used to holding against the spring on upward changes from second to third and all changes between third and fourth you soon appreciated how well it worked, as in traffic you frequently want first or second gear very quickly and this spring biasing system put the lever ready to select either extremely rapidly.

These gearboxes lasted well except for the reverse idler gear which can easily be abused and then cause a failure. Late in the models' production run, this was upgraded with a new, very durable gear made under part number EN618571 which should be fitted any time a gearbox is being serviced. (This gear can also be fitted to the 16/18hp synchromesh gearbox). Like any gearboxes they can suffer from stupidity and misuse, but when used in a proper way they have a long life with 100,000 miles without overhaul not being uncommon.

On the top of the gearbox is located a switch operated by the selector rods to control automatically the reverse light and another switch for the overdrive lockout if overdrive is fitted. The lower casing of the gearbox is externally finned for cooling.

It is not possible to state accurately how many of each type of transmission arrangement was built as about 50% of all the car files are now lost as are a number of the car cards and in some cases the gearbox type serial number was not entered on the card.

Both the 234 and the 236 were available with the proven Laycock de Normanville type A overdrive. Whilst the overdrive units appear to be identical for the 234 and the 236 they are in fact set up differently to accommodate the torque outputs and power curves of the two different engines, and to further complicate the matter Manumatic 236s use yet another variant. Serial numbers are recorded in Appendix 20.

On 236 cars fitted with both Manumatic and overdrive the ability to use overdrive third was not offered. Cars with the conventional clutch – both 234s and 236s – always have overdrive operating on both top and third gear when fitted.

The overdrive is electrically engaged by a selector switch mounted on the column beneath the steering wheel and its operation is controlled by a bulkhead mounted relay, protected by a fuse, which feeds an engagement solenoid on the side of the overdrive unit.

The overdrive is, in my opinion, a must, as it transforms the car into an effortless cruiser for long distance work and the big plus is a fuel saving of about 7 miles per gallon for such fast touring. Third gear and overdrive third are ideal for mounting climbing, turning passes into sheer driving fun.

The precise number of cars fitted with overdrive is unknown, however the writer's estimate, based on a variety of data sources, would indicate that about 25% of all 236s and about 50% of all 234s were originally so equipped. Quite a number of cars have had overdrives fitted in later life, either at a factory service depot or dealer, and in some cases overdrives from accident damaged cars have been fitted by enthusiastic owners. It would seem that the overdrive was viewed sceptically by many new car purchasers, but the reliability of the unit and its general acceptance has grown in later years to make it *the* desired extra.

The 234 and 236 share the same type propeller shaft, significantly shorter than that of the 346 and hence with no centre bearing. The shaft length was shorter for two reasons; firstly the wheelbase was already 3in shorter and secondly the overdrive (or gearbox extension if not fitted with overdrive) added considerably to the length from the back of the engine to the drive take off-point. The shaft is the typical Hardy Spicer type with a sliding coupling at the front and two standard universal joints, one at each end.

Both the 234 and the 236 share the same basic rear axle and differential assembly. This unit was again bought out and came from the Salisbury company, being of the same family as all the postwar models but a lighter item designed for a smaller car. It was Salisbury type 3HA, also found on 2.4 Jaguars and some Daimler Conquests, and while satisfactory, was not as durable as the 2HA and 4HA units fitted to the larger cars.

The 3HA unit tends to be somewhat hard on ball and roller races and unless new races are fitted to about every 60,000-75,000 miles a failure can easily occur: when a race fails it usually results in a major differential failure. The Salisbury company soon found out this problem and offered a heavier duty derivative known as the 7HA which was fitted to the last of the Daimler Conquests. Owners would be well advised to seek out the various items that upgrade a 3HA unit to the 7HA specification and modify their cars accordingly. I am informed that the only changes are within the standard diff housing and concern the carrier, sun and star gears. Naturally the 234s are more likely to have a differential failure as they have almost 50% more power to deal with than the 236s. This is a word of warning, but to counter the argument, I also know of a 236 with almost 300,000 miles to its credit using its original differential which has remained untouched from new.

Wheels, tyres and hubcaps

The 234/236 cars came with standard steel pressed wheels, with five-stud fixing. An option offered was knock-off wire wheels; as already mentioned only the 234 was actually fitted with wire wheels in production. After a fairly unsuccessful initial reaction to wire wheels, 234 buyers started to realize how attractive they looked and by the last year of production a significant proportion were leaving the factory with this option. This change of attitude reflects the fact that the more sporting buyer had discovered by this time what the 234 really was – a sports car in saloon car clothing.

The standard bolt-on disc wheel is of 15in diameter, with 5in width rims of the K type, manufactured by Dunlop. This wheel was normally fitted with 640x15 cross-ply tyres, usually of Dunlop manufacture. Once radial tyres became available in the late 1950s some cars started to be fitted with 175x15 Michelin or Pirelli tyres; these dramatically improve road holding and cornering while lightening steering effort.

The hubcaps for these wheels are identical to the 346 limousine and Star limousine hubcap, being a fairly simple chrome dome type which had the inscription 'Armstrong Siddeley' pressed in a circle into the central area. The standard wheels fitted with the standard hubcap look a fairly drab affair and this caused many owners to have their wheels fitted with dress rings or Rimbellishers which dramatically improved the appearance. The standard factory option were wide style Ace Rimbellishers which were secured from inside the wheel by screwed anchorage clips. The wheels were always painted to match the body colour of the car.

Bodywork

The 234/236 body was an entirely new concept for Armstrong Siddeley, their first full-width body and a modern slippery shape, rather than one derived from traditional coachbuilt forms like its big brother. It was made deliberately light in weight, for an Armstrong Siddeley, and used, like the Whitley, a combination of both alloy and steel panel work. The body was fully fabricated in metal and used no structural woodwork. The only woodwork was internal and strictly ornamental.

The body had a basic steel shell comprising pressed steel wheelarches, bulkhead, inner mudguard panels and door frames. The balance was built of an aircraft high duty alloy known as Hiduminium 22. The main components made from this metal were

Both 234/236 and 346 Sapphires are to be seen taking shape in this photograph of the Armstrong Siddeley body-building shop at the Parkside factory during 1957. The two types were built together on a batch basis, the lack of a separate production facility for the smaller model limiting the numbers that could be made.

doorskins, turret, boot and bonnet surrounds, door sills, and floor. The bootlid was initially made of Hiduminium but was not found to be satisfactory in this material: no doubt due to its size and shape, it was soon to become a composite steel pressing.

The bumper bars were pressed by the Templewood Engineering company who were within the Hawker Siddeley group. These are two-piece bars joined centrally, as again it was envisaged that often half a bumper bar would be required for repair in the average collision. These are very easy to change over.

The doors were designed to eliminate the lovely chrome frame tops as used in all other postwar Armstrong models. The windows had a simple chrome clip-in surround much the same as Rovers, Singers and Humbers of the period had; while the system worked well, it certainly cheapened the side appearance. Each of the four doors was able to be opened up to a full 90-degree angle providing easy ingress and egress.

The light nature of these bodies proved to be both a blessing and a curse. So good was the design that they gave absolutely no structural problems, even after extended outback use, but being of a thin section, the steel was easily attacked by rust when they were used in salty road conditions and quite early in their life some bodies started to deteriorate. The conditions in England were such that rust free examples are now hard to find, whereas those few that did reach Australia have stood up extraordinarily well because the fundamental body design was so functional. It is indeed a pity that such a splendid car could not have been protected from rust by the processes we have today.

The appearance of the body is quite unusual and not to everybody's liking. It was almost certainly far too modern for its era, particularly when you think of the conservative period in which it was released and the tradional clientele Armstrong Siddeley had previously espoused. I think it would be fair to say that it belongs to the 1960s design school rather than the mid 1950s.

The car has a somewhat high roofline, and the story goes that an executive director of Armstrong Siddeley Motors, Mr Ashley, complained that he couldn't sit with his Homburg hat in place in the back seat of the prototype and insisted that the roofline be raised; most people believe that this was the main reason the roofline looks somewhat heavy. Appearance-wise this is certainly a pity, but from inside the high seating and splendid visibility for all passengers, particularly those in the back seat, is one of the car's best features.

The 234/236 body was exhaustively tested and was designed to have, for those days, a low drag coefficient, though the figure was never recorded or perhaps not even determined. The body is almost turbulence free and this characteristic is most evident at, say, 80mph in overdrive top where it wafts along in near total silence.

The body's designers called for easy removal and replacement of all four mudguards in the event of a collision. This concept was largely lost in execution as the factory would never risk anything coming loose, so they bolted the mudguards on very fully, making them not much easier to remove than on any previous model.

The 234/236 was the first postwar Armstrong Siddeley to have all

four doors front hung, increasing safety though at some cost to ease of ingress and egress. Other safety features included cast variable strength bonnet hinges, that were designed to break off in the unlikely event of the bonnet coming open at speed. This enables the bonnet to become a type of airfoil and become airborne from its opening so it would float over the roof and windscreen without touching either. One enthusiastic owner had this unnerving experience and was relieved to see the bonnet land gently on the road behind her – another owner had a similar experience only to have a truck run over the errant panel! Another nice safety feature is the quite outstanding forward vision. There is also the windscreen which is designed, like the 346, to pop out if a person's body is thrown against it. There are other niceties such as child-proof door locks for the rear doors, not a common feature of this period.

Of all the considerable number of cars that the writer has owned, the 234/236 body has been found to be the one that best stays rattle free, and this, together with its exceptional leg and arm room, makes it a joy to use. Its design was an entirely in-house production and no doubt more of a committee effort than the work of a gifted stylist: perhaps that is why it features a high level of function, rather than typifying everybody's idea of what an Armstrong Siddeley should look like.

The body was painted in nitrocellulose lacquers of Pinchin and Johnson manufacture and was very well finished in detail, being entirely 'orange peel' free. It used a colour range that incorporated some colours new to Armstrong Siddeley and re-used those that were deemed suitable from the existing range. Much experimentation was done with two tone paintwork on prototypes and eventually it was decided to offer the roof in an alternative colour, should the owner so choose; however the problem of where to finish the second

140

colour at the front of the turret caused much discussion and experimentation. Eventually the factory selected an angular cut-off down the windscreen posts which worked out well and looked appropriate. The colours were as follows: Ivory; Eau de Nil (light green, usually a roof colour); Corinthian Green (dark green, 346 colour); Ashley Blue (mid/dark blue, usually a roof colour, probably named after the person who wanted the roof height increased); Powder Blue; Langham Grey (a soft green grey, first used on the Whitleys, also a 346 colour); and Black.

The 234/236 interior was somewhat less elaborate than that of its bigger brother. It featured twin front bucket seats with high-backed squabs. These seats were identical to the optional bucket seats for the 346 Sapphire but were trimmed differently; after the first thousand seats there was a minor design change for the remaining production run. Turning to the generous rear seat, this had, as usual, a folding central arm rest, and could comfortably accommodate three adults as it was wider than the 346 seat. These seats were trimmed mainly with ICI vinyl (Vyanide VT1175) with the exception of woven nylon inserts for both cushion and squabs. This nylon material looked most attractive and was designed to breathe, but its life was relatively short at about 60,000 miles of use. A few examples were supplied in full leather trim which could be ordered as an extra but was only supplied if a customer enquired about it, as it was not featured on the sales brochure. The standard interior colour selection was grey, blue, green, red, beige and (occasionally) brown.

The factory brochure suggests that certain exterior colours were intended to go with their predetermined choice of interior colour, but, while this was largely adhered to, there were many cars supplied by the factory with differing arrangements to those shown on the brochure. The headlining was the usual standard Armstrong Siddeley ivory material, while the carpet was identical to the material in the 346 Sapphire and was always supplied to match the seat colour.

Polished woodwork of the straight grain style was provided on the instrument panel and door cappings to similar standard to that fitted to the Whitley. The instrument panel central section varied as the 234 models incorporated a centrally mounted tachometer, while the 236 panel had an ultraviolet-lit central switch panel in lieu. These instrument panels are unusual in design and quite attractive. The central grouping of the instruments and switches resulted in the cluster of four small instruments being not in a direct line of sight for the driver. There were two small glove boxes, one at each end, neither of which was supplied with a lid. All polished woodwork was beautifully finished and became one of the main features of the car's interior.

Overall the car's interior appearance was attractive, very functional and in good taste; it lacked the traditional Armstrong Siddeley looks but not comfort as the ergonomic design of the seats and arm rests was of a high order. The door trims were plain and functional, all four doors had adjustable arm rests, while the driver's door window was raised and lowered by a quick-action lift mechanism.

The floor of the car was largely flat excepting a small transmission tunnel in the rear and a fairly usual hump over the gearbox. The floor layout and body proportions were such that all passengers had exceptional leg and knee room. With the high roof line all four or five passengers sat in an elevated position in great comfort with remarkable visibility.

The engine compartment was entirely different to any previous model and somewhat similar to the larger Austin-Healeys, with a front-opening hatch type lid and a fixed bonnet surround panel. There were two different under bonnet arrangements. The first 703 bodies had angular fabricated inner front mudguard panels, and from body number 180704 these panels were significantly changed to a simple flat form. This resulted in some repositioning of ancillary components, heater ducting, etc. Accessibility was reasonable for service, while engine removal and replacement was far easier than it looked.

The most disappointing feature of the car is the relatively modest boot. I believe the available space could have been better used if the spare wheel had been lowered and a hinged floor incorporated. It is rather surprising that Armstrong Siddeley produced such a layout, especially as the prototype and possibly a handful of the early production cars had a different floor arrangement which was redesigned but still only produced a moderately satisfactory boot in its final form. This boot continued the concept of the flat storage of the spare wheel with a compartment for tools beside it, and a useful trough was also incorporated in much the same way as the Whitley and 346 Sapphire. The small tools were packed in an identical tool roll to the Whitley with identical tools for the 236 and only a changed spark plug spanner for the 234. The standard boot was a austerely fitted out with the normal wicker-patterned floor mat.

The body was basically identical for both the 234 and 236 models but there were a number of minor differences as demanded, such as the changed centre instrument panel, bracketing for the 236 Manumatic controls, etc. All bodies were designed to accommodate right or lefthand drive, the only variation being which side front door had the quick-action window lift.

During the three years plus of the models' production there were scarcely any bodywork changes, other than already mentioned; those changes that did occur were of an extremely minor nature, such as the front bumper aprons being fitted with and without wing piping.

There were three non-standard 234/236 bodies built, two being in-house designs and the other being an attractive body by Michelotti for a Spanish customer.

The first special body was a 234 sports roadster, details of which are no longer available. It is thought to be chassis 4230170 and probably only reached the prototype stage. Chassis 4230566 with a complete body was supplied to the experimental department, devoid of any paint. It is thought that this particular vehicle was probably the one that was made into the utility, as we know at least one car was converted for evaluation along the lines of the 346 pick-up that was produced for the oil companies – a cheaply printed brochure still

Three photographs dated March 27, 1958, of the unique Michelotti bodied 234 Sapphire, chassis C4230551. The car was registered in Madrid the same month but further details of its ownership or ultimate fate are unknown. The integration of a traditional grille into the contemporary frontal styling is successful enough even if its specific Armstrong Siddeley identity is not very strong.

exists for this vehicle.

Another mystery consists of chassis 4230565 which was fitted with a standard body painted Langham Grey, but no engine. This was no doubt fitted with a high performance experimental engine for testing, and may well have had modifications to the body to take a Star or 346 engine.

The Michelotti-bodied car was a special order for a customer whose name does not appear to be recorded. It was built on a 234 lefthand-drive chassis, 4230551, which was the only one to be supplied to an outside coachbuilder. Many people have tried to locate this car, but to date its whereabouts or final fate remain a mystery; all that we have been able to find out is that it was first registered in Madrid in March 1958. Your author, for one, would dearly like to learn more about this interesting car.

On the road
Conservative people who did not find the appearance of these cars to their liking, often passed them over and did not properly evaluate the 234/236 range. If these people had road tested one, they would surely have formed other ideas and come to value the cars for what they really are – a superb handling, quiet and tractable package. A point not properly appreciated was that the two cars had entirely different characteristics.

The 234 was 5-6cwt lighter than its bigger brother the 346 but had

Instrument panel and controls of a 234 Sapphire: note the prominent central rev counter, evidence of the sporty nature of the car's power unit, and the overdrive switch to the right of the steering column. The addition of overdrive made the 234 a very capable long-distance high-speed cruiser.

only 5bhp less, a combination which made the car a real flyer. The four-cylinder engine revved very well and was effective and safe to 5,500rpm. With the car's aerodynamic shape and taut suspension, this engine, coupled with the sweet synchromesh gearbox, meant that you had nothing short of a sports car, appearances notwithstanding. The Laycock de Normanville overdrive was really a must; cars fitted with overdrive would cruise at 100mph in an uncanny way. You could, as with all Armstrong Siddeley cars, cover huge mileages in a day, yet the 234 would yield up to 28mpg if driven carefully or 22-24mpg if enthusiastically driven.

The 234 has consequently often been described as a wolf in sheep's clothing, a highway eater and yet docile in traffic. Enthusiasts are advised to try and acquire one – a task that won't be easy as there are relatively few good 234s left: they seem to have suffered a very different fate to the 236 as they attracted a totally different original purchaser and many of them have by now been used so much that their mechanical components need major rebuilding. To restore such a car is a very worthwhile task, resulting in a classic car with almost totally modern handling and performance. If, that is, you can find one which, perhaps because it has been kept in a kind climate, has not succumbed to the ravages of rust.

The 236, on the other hand, is quite a different car, although sharing the same body and chassis; its engine is a silky smooth six that is nothing more than a higher performance version of the earlier 18hp unit. The 236 is about $2\frac{1}{2}$cwt lighter than, say, a Whitley, and has 10 extra bhp in engine performance. This, coupled with a higher ratio differential, makes the car relatively fast but not brisk. Its performance at lower speed levels is somewhat leisurely, but is still very pleasant and acceptable; once you build up engine and road speed, the car changes its character and becomes a sweet touring car of ample performance.

Many original owners were sold their 236s for town and traffic use, thus only a relatively small proportion are fitted with overdrive and a great many are fitted with the Manumatic clutch. This is a great pity as the overdrive top gear makes open road touring in the 80-85mph speed range very pleasant with the smooth engine just quietly humming away.

The Manumatic clutch control gave two-pedal motoring, yet in many ways eliminated the problems associated with an automatic gearbox when coupled to a small capacity engine. All the driver had to do was move the gearlever and the Manumatic control looked after everything, making the car as agile as a normal manual car, yet foolproof and easy to drive – as the gearbox itself was such a joy, it was no chore to use. Probably the rarest 236 combination is a car with a standard clutch and an overdrive. The records show, however, quite a number were built. In cars 2360443 and 2360445 your writer has done a great deal of driving, much of it in the outback, and I found the 236 a satisfactory and enjoyable car, even if a little bit down in performance. On rough, unmade roads both the 234s and 236s endeared themselves to me, as they revel in coping with stones, potholes and corrugated gravel surfaces, the car's long suspension travel being ideal for such use, and good visibility over the sloping bonnet enables one to place the car accurately in some of the worst so-called 'road' situations.

The 234 and 236 Sapphires must be among the most under-appreciated cars ever to have been produced, technically and practically successful yet largely overlooked. It is a great pity so few were produced and, further to compound this shortage today, so few were exported to the drier climates where rust has not ruined them. I doubt if more than 350 of the 1,506 remain today, yet in Australia we still have 7 out of the 9 cars that reached us.

Tool kit supplied as standard for the 236 and all later 18hp cars. For the 234, the kit was the same except for the substitution of the long spark plug spanner also supplied for the 346 and Star.

Modifications

The 234/236 had relatively few modifications during the three-year production run. The following list covers the main changes that occurred. As some are applicable to chassis, some to body and some to the two different engines, I list them together: in many cases they interrelate. You will note that only the 'class A' 234 engine change and the bodywork changes to the inner mudguard panels are of any real significance. Modifications relate to both 234 and 236 except where specifically designated.

Chassis 230251 New type rear stabilizer bar and fittings.

Body 180416 New front bumper valance at 230399 for 236 and 4230032 for 234.

Chassis 230501 New upgraded steering centre idler.

Body 180704 Entirely new inner front mudguard panel, revised bulkhead, battery repositioned and other changes to make engine bay more accessible.

Gearbox 2301001 Casing upgraded and other minor modifications.

Body 181001 New air scoop to radiator.

Body 181001 Revised front bucket seats and runners.

Body 181001 Reinforced inner front mudguard panels.

Body 181201 New reverse idler introduced to gearbox.

After first 40 cars (234 only) Class A modification: after experience in service, it was indicated that engines ran too hot and failed to idle smoothly – thus a warranty change was ordered for all cars already sold and for all cars to be built in the future. The changes were: (**a**) camshaft with less overlap; (**b**) five-row radiator in lieu of four-row type; (**c**) fitment of seven-bladed fan and cowl; (**d**) changed carburettor needles; (**e**) valve springs fitted with spacer washers; (**f**) gearbox judder ring removed; (**g**) modified rear engine mount; (**h**) engine to be stamped **C** on the offside of the horizontal section of the block at rear of timing chest (denoting modifications have been carried out); (**i**) new type fan pulley. First standard engine to be built to this revised specification numbered E2340041.

Engine 2340501 (234 only) New valve spring collars introduced.

Chassis 4230501 (234 only) New rear road springs introduced.

Chassis 4230579 (234 only) New, improved distributor fitted.

Chassis 4230587 (234 only) Clayton Dewandre brake servo replaced by Girling Mark 2 unit.

Chassis 4230727 (234 only) New brake fluid reservoir introduced.

Engine 2360501 (236 only) New rear main bearing cap and new thrust bearing cap introduced in crankcase.

234/236 facts

The first 234/236 chassis built was S230001 being finished on October 21, 1955. This was the 236 Coventry demonstrator, registration number RVC 906.

The first 234/236 body built (180001) was fitted to 236 chassis 230002.

The first 236 chassis had body 180004 (the fourth built).

The first 234 was chassis F230004 and was also a Coventry demonstrator, coming on to fleet on January 3, 1956, registration number SDU 666.

The last 234 chassis (4230803) had body 181404 being completed on October 15, 1958.

Chassis F230065 had a 234 experimental engine number EX234/4 fitted.

Chassis 230586 had a steering column one inch longer than the standard item, presumably a special request from its purchaser.

There were 29 cars produced with the non-standard colour scheme of powder blue with Sapphire blue roof.

Optional extras listed for both models were: laminated windscreen (a requirement in some countries); Armstrong brand heavy duty shock absorbers; seven-bladed fan for 236; wheel dress rings (Rimbellishers) for disc wheels; wire wheels (painted in body colour or silver metallic, or fully chrome plated); thief-proof petrol filler pipe; rear mudguard stone protectors (chrome over cast brass); oil-bath air cleaners (mostly standard on export cars); radio (usually HMV): wing mirrors; and fog and long range driving lights (either SLR/SFT 576 or SLR/STF 700).

Extras available to special order included leather interior trim; heavy-duty rear springs; adjustable ride rear shock absorbers; an interior coat rail; non-standard paint; and a radiator blind.

5

Polishing the gem

The Star Sapphire, 1958 to 1960

By 1957 the sales of the 346 Sapphire had started to wane, the 236 Sapphire had failed to sell at the expected level and the 234 Sapphire was just starting to be accepted, with sales increasing. Clearly, there was room for a new model.

At this time the group's corporate resources were stretched to the limit in the more lucrative aviation and engineering areas. Yet the design office for the car section still had capacity, and were busy designing a new model, firstly intended for release in late 1958, later revised to 1960. Unfortunately the corporate board could not allocate capital and engineering resources to have the new car ready for the market by 1960, and shelved it for a further two years, targeting a release date for the Motor Show late in 1962.

That postponement of the completely new model forced Armstrong Siddeley Motors to rethink its strategy, and it was decided that they would engage in a stopgap approach and rework the highly successful 346 Sapphire into a far more luxurious vehicle. The engineering and design departments were then given the task of making a new derivative that would raise further the standard of what had become one of the great luxury saloons of the decade. In colloquial terms they were asked 'to trump their own ace'.

The factory owned a 346 Sapphire which was used as a mobile test bed; every innovation and design change was tried out on that car, so little by little it became less and less a modified 346 and more and more the new variant, which we later came to know as the Star Sapphire.

The changes became so numerous that the Star was, in fact, almost an entirely new car. The only panels that interchanged in the end were the bootlid, scuttle/bulkhead, rear wheelarches, and inner front mudguard panels; even the turret was marginally changed around the rear quarter lights! The interior appointments were all new excepting the door linings' basic design. Mechanically the car had a smoother larger engine, new automatic gearbox, changed differential ratio, changes to the front suspension, and disc front brakes were introduced along with a power steering system, with a power boosted steering box rather than the earlier external ram. These changes and improvements were complemented by a greater level of luxury in equipment.

During the development process, the mobile test bed, registered TDU 707, became known to all as the Star Sapphire. It was driven day in, day out and also most nights, either on the MIRA test track or up and down the highways and byways, until it was virtually perfect. Never before had an Armstrong Siddeley car gone through such development work prior to public release. Not that this stopped on release: it was continued, and when the M1 motorway was opened, the car was driven up and down the stretch from Coventry to London, with a team of drivers, for destruction-testing at up to 100mph for 24 hours per day, week in, week out, as previously no such opportunity had existed in England for such prolonged high-speed testing. During the post-release M1 testing, it was found that the engine oil temperature in flat-out motoring continued to rise to uncomfortable levels, so late in 1959 a variety of minor modifications were introduced. These included a special wider cast engine sump, with the return oil passed around the enlarged perimeter prior to re-use. This change made a considerable difference and kept the oil far cooler. At the time of cessation of manufacture TDU 707 had covered in excess of 250,000 miles and even been test crashed into the only tree at the MIRA test ground at about 80mph. This unique car still survives, having now done at least 400,000 miles.

Interestingly, TDU 707 was cleaned up and made to look like a new car and took its place beside the first production Star, chassis 330001, at that Motor Show. The press and public were unaware that it had started its life as a normal 346 Sapphire and was really a very used car. It was kept for use by the chief engineer, Mr Alex Rice, until 1962 or 1963 when he purchased it from the company for his private use. Today it still belongs to one of his sons, Mr Steven Rice, and has undergone its first major full restoration – what a car to own!

At the Motor Show in October 1958 this revised stopgap model was released to the public who reacted very favourably. The show organisers were so impressed with its finish that the Star was

Armstrong Siddeley Star Sapphire, superficially similar to the previous 346 model but actually the product of a comprehensive programme of development and refinement which resulted in what was in effect a completely new car. This is the second example built, chassis 330002, much road tested by the motoring writers of the era.

awarded the Gold Medal and first prize of the Institute of British Carriage and Automobile Manufacturers for cars priced between £1,300 and £4,000 (excluding purchase tax). This award was quite an achievement.

While the Star Sapphire at first glance looks very similar to the earlier 346 models, it repays very close inspection, as the multiplicity of changes and improvements produced what was, in effect, an entirely new car. To drive a Star is a new experience; the car feels smaller, is more manoeuvrable and far more docile, yet has outstanding performance, particularly in the 60 to 90mph speed range. *Autosport* magazine managed to obtain a standing quarter mile figure of 18.2 seconds, which is still a good figure today, and only a few luxury saloons were that quick in 1958. It was not until the horsepower race of the later 1960s that the Star's performance was overshadowed. Being a 35½cwt car with a 4-litre engine and automatic gearbox, it could not complete in the cubic capacity stakes for brute power; but still even 30 years after its release, it is able to acquit itself particularly well in city traffic and fast motorway use. With the end of the horsepower race and the return to more manageable sized cars, the Star today is up to all that is required by 99% of highway drivers.

Your author has owned a number of Star Sapphires and has done at least 100,000 miles in them and they are, in my opinion, the greatest of all Armstrong Siddeley cars. When *Wheels* magazine road tested Star 330010 in Melbourne their headline was 'The final polish for an old Gem'.

The Star was initially only offered in saloon form and the 346 Sapphire limousine continued for nearly another 14 months before a

Marsden's superb drawing of the Star Sapphire chassis for *The Autocar* was used for publicity purposes by Armstrong Siddeley and clearly illustrates the salient technical features of the design.

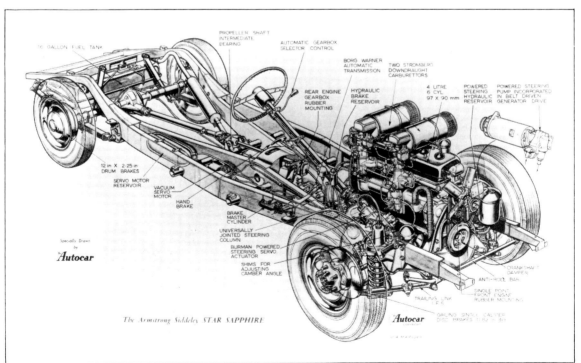

Extensive and elaborate testing went into the development of the car and continued even after its launch: these factory photographs date from 1959. Left, Star Sapphire chassis 330001 on a suspension proving rig at the Parkside plant, and above, the same vehicle undergoing electronic engine performance checks.

Star limousine became available. There was no four-light body option nor were any utilities, sports cars or other derivatives offered. There was no choice of gearbox as, alas, the market of the day in luxury cars wanted only automatic. So the faithful preselective gearbox was no longer built. It is understood that the experimental department converted one or perhaps two for customers or staff to preselective gears, but none have turned up of recent years.

Strangely, the limousine version when introduced for the start of 1960 had a standard synchromesh gearbox, the automatic being an option at an extra cost. This was possibly done to suit the hire-car operators rather than the owner driver. Of the 77 limousine chassis built, only 12 had automatic gearboxes.

The single Star saloon prototype was, as already explained, a modified 346 chassis, fitted with experimental ·engine EX/97/12. There followed a total of 902 production Star Sapphire saloons, chassis numbers 330001 to 330902. Development of the limousines version involved two prototypes, chassis numbers 40001 and 40002. Star limousine production chassis numbers ran from 36003 to 360073, a total of 71 cars, and there were a further four long chassis allocated for special coachwork, numbers 360074 to 360077. Total production of all variants, therefore, was 980.

The chassis frame

The chassis frame was very similar to the 346 chassis but there were a number of modifications mainly in the central X-bracing area, with entirely new gearbox mountings. These were fixed in position thus eliminating the separate rear mounting towers, problems that beset roughly used and high mileage 346s; however, the trade-off for this improvement was the inability to remove the gearbox for service without taking out the engine and gearbox as one unit.

The rear spring mountings were modified for the short or saloon chassis and totally changed on the long or limousine chassis. There were other modifcations of a fairly minor nature, to accommodate a revised master cylinder mounting, brake hose anchorage, steering

Star Sapphire chassis being assembled at the factory in 1959: careful batch building rather than mass production on a moving line. The chassis nearest the camera, awaiting its engine and gearbox, still has spring compressors attached to the front suspension.

box mounting and other various fittings, as although the car was mechanically quite similar, it was, in fact, significantly changed and with these changes there were a multiplicity of minor modifications.

The modified chassis frame was fitted with the (by now) stiffened front suspension crossmember, which was already well tested on later 346s. This had different locating mountings for the upper inner suspension pivot which was significantly improved. The chassis with its heavier duty suspension crossmember was quite robust and gave no problems in service.

The suspension and steering

Once again, this system was very similar in basic layout and design to the 346 models; however there were a number of changes. The front suspension used the late 346 type crossmember, lower wishbones, lower pivots, etc. The upper wishbones were modified to accommodate the car's smaller turning circle, and the upper inner pivots were now provided with a shim system to enable the housing and its adjustable shaft to be accurately positioned to give both castor and camber adjustments for steering geometry.

With the inclusion of disc brakes came a new front hub and stub axle which enabled the wheels to be mounted with a wider track; this significantly reduced turning circle, now down to 37ft. All the lessons learnt with the 346 were automatically incorporated into the Star's production from the first car and no modifications of any note took place during its production run.

The Star saloon followed the same basic rear suspension arrangement as the 346 Sapphire, but with detailed differences. The semi-elliptical springs were designed to run in a nearly flat plane with little curvature being evident once they had settled down after a few weeks of use. To accommodate this arrangement, the rear shackle eye mounting was lowered to below the chassis frame, in place of the 346's through mounting arrangement. This gave the car a lower setting for the rear body in relation to the ground, thus eliminating the slightly front down look sometimes seen on the 346s.

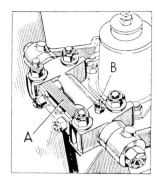

Close-up of the inner pivot of the upper wishbone showing, A, the shims which could be added or removed to adjust the suspension geometry and B, the lubricator to allow oil (not grease) to be supplied to the bearing.

The vertical movement was limited by a new large D-shaped pierced bump stop which allowed a progressive retardation of the axle when approaching the limit of upwards travel. On initial contact it would absorb 30lb of load and worked up to 1,000lb under full compression. This progressive rubber limit buffer was manufactured by Dunlop's Metalastik Division.

The Star limousine, developed later than the saloon, had the benefit of both the experience gained and changing technology. The rear springs, while still of the semi-elliptical type, were rather differently mounted. The conventional rear spring shackles were deleted in favour of a somewhat strange rear end box, on which were mounted two laminated metal and rubber sandwich bobbin type mounts at an angle. This arrangement positioned the rear end of the springs far more accurately. It worked well and gave the limousine a quieter and better ride. Incidentally this system was to have been adopted for the Mark 2 saloon chassis when produced, and did find its way onto the prototype, saloon chassis 330905.

The Star underwent a significant change from the 346 in the steering box and column. The Star was equipped with a Burman power steering box and a separate column, coupled via a rubber bushed semi-universal joint, which provided insulation from any stray road shocks. The steering linkage from the steering box was by way of similar (but modified) pitman arm and its drag link to the centre idler. The tie rods were shortened to couple to modified steering arms as part of the redesign to decrease the turning circle.

The power steering box was boosted by a Hoburn Eaton hydraulic pump, mounted on the aft end of the generator; twin fan belts were incorporated to take the extra load. The separate hydraulic reservoir and its filter were mounted on the chassis by a bracket near the corner of the engine compartment.

The steering wheel was changed from the traditional immediately postwar style to a far more modern two-spoke type with a large centre boss and cowl. The new wheel had a central horn push, while the direction indicator switch was side mounted and self cancelling

153

in the modern manner. The steering wheel was still adjustable for reach; its control was by way of a 'ship's wheel' type adjuster lock nut, accessed under the cowl, which gave the user about 3in of movement.

These modifcations and improvements made the Star a different car to use; it was so light to steer and so manoeuvrable with its reduced turning circle that it felt nimble and effortless to drive. Some drivers found the steering too light, and it seems that way as you move from a non-assisted car into the Star. However, it soon feels ideal for the driver after it is used for a few miles, making the car feel particularly well balanced. In service these power steering components have all been relatively trouble free and have required little more than the occasional seal or O-ring replacement.

The Star was fitted with tubular shock absorbers in the same way as the 346 and 234/6 models, either of Girling or Armstrong manufacture; both proved satisfactory and long lasting, with the Girling brand being the better for Australian use. Most UK-delivered cars seem to have had the softer riding Armstrong brand fitted as original equipment. Modern gas shock absorbers were not available at the time the car was produced, but by fitting the Koni gas type now available you can improve the ride and handling significantly.

The brakes
The Star saloon was the first production Armstrong Siddeley to incorporate disc brakes and like so many cars had discs at the front and drums at the rear. The system was of Girling manufacture. Apart from the discs and a separate vacuum reservoir, the installation was again virtually the same as the late Mark 2 346 Sapphires. The 12in diameter reinforced discs were of the non-ventilated type, operated by a Girling type 18 double piston caliper. At the rear, 12in diameter finned drums contained one leading and one trailing shoe per brake. The handbrake operated on the rear wheels only by mechanical and cable linkage, from a pistol grip under the dash. The brake boost was provided by a Girling vacuum servo. Initially cars had the Mark 1 booster but during the production run the Mark 2 version became available and was immediately incorporated. The master cylinder was of 0.875in bore, working a single system.

The brakes as fitted worked particularly well, even by today's standards,and at release must have been quite outstanding when compared with many other cars. The system has proven itself to need only the usual routine attention and overhauls after long lengths of service. If used particularly hard, the brakes are found to be virtually fade free and cope with arresting the car's considerable mass with ease – even when applied at 100mph.

Owners using a Star on unmade roads and stony conditions were advised to fit a metal protective shield to stop stone damage to the master cylinder; a similar shield should be fitted to the servo booster when used in such conditions.

Two types of handbrake lever were fitted. The first,and by far the more common,was a repeat of the pistol grip type of the 16/18hp and 346 Sapphires, but this time painted black, rather than brown.

However, a twist D-grip chrome plated lever was also offered and became standard issue on cars going to the Canary Islands, Holland, Portugal, Canada, Saudi Arabia, USA, Sweden and Switzerland.

The long-chassis Star limousine's brakes are an interesting combination of items from other models. The front disc brakes follow exactly the pattern of the Star saloon, while the rear drum brakes are reduced in diameter from 12in to 11in and use the Mark 1 346 Sapphire system with later wheel cylinders. Again the entire system is of Girling manufacture.

The reason for this change is that the Star limousine had 15in diameter road wheels and the 12in brake set could not be accommodated within the available space. No doubt it was felt that the limousine would not be as fast as the saloon nor as enthusiastically driven. Yet although the car's mass was greater, these brakes worked very well and were still well up to the job as demanded. There were only minor changes from the saloon otherwise except that the factory standardized on the D-twist grip handbrake lever, abandoning the pistol grip type after 15 years of successful service.

The engine

The six-cylinder in-line engine for the Star was a much worked-over version of the 346 engine. It was bored out to 97mm but retained the 90mm stroke, the cubic capacity rising from 3,435cc to 3,990cc (virtually 4 litres). This became the first and only production Armstrong Siddeley to be of the 'over square' configuration. With this change were a plethora of minor revisions and improvements, so much so that while its heritage is obvious, there is very little interchangeability.

New were the engine block, cylinder head, crankshaft, camshaft, con rods (ex 234), pistons, valves, bearings, timing chain (with a hydraulic tensioner for the first time), flywheel, sump, rocker cover, inlet manifolds, twin carburettors, air cleaners, etc. The brake horsepower only rose to 165 from the 150 of the twin carburettor 346, but at the lower figure of 4,250rpm rather than 5,000rpm for the 346. However, the real change was an increase in torque by 38lb/ft at the same 2,000rpm engine speed as before.

The Star's engine block was completely new. The larger bore necessitated moving the cylinder line 0.1in away from the crankshaft centre line. This had the effect of reducing the side thrust of the pistons on the power stroke. The later Star engines also had enlarged water jackets by modifying the righthand side of the block and fitting two oblong cover plates.

Heavier duty connecting rods and bearings were like those introduced for the 234 engine, while a less extreme camshaft profile was employed to give very smooth idling and torque delivery. This no doubt robbed the Star of some potential top-end sparkle but made it a very tractable engine to give the car even more effortless highway performance. Other factors like the incorporation of large diameter manifolding and ports, bigger valves etc, all played their part. One can't help wondering what sort of highway eater a Star engine would have been with a high lift sporting 346 camshaft and the early 346

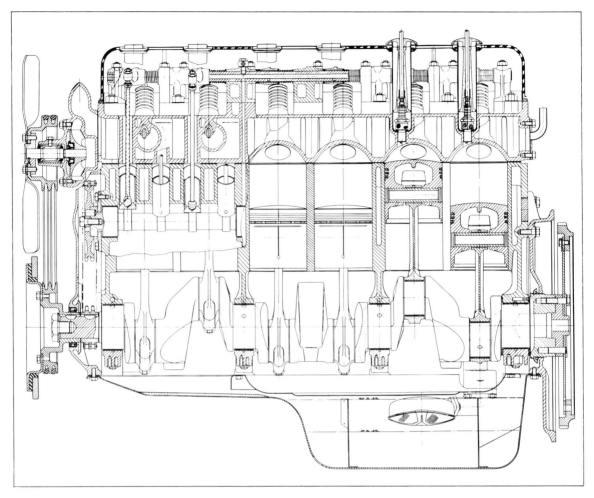

Longitudinal section of the Star Sapphire engine revealing some of the technical details of its construction. Though based on the preceding 346 engine, this unit had many revised components including the cylinder block and the major moving parts.

distributor, the latter having a more radical advance curve – we will probably never know! In the event, it proved to be a far more flexible engine with effortless power. The Star will romp up almost any hill, even with its automatic gearbox which, as usual with this type of transmission, significantly robs power. Oh for a preselective gearbox Star!

During the production run of the Star engine there were a number of improvements made, occasioned by the implemention of test feedback from the endless M1 motorway testing. These changes resulted in increased water ways in the block, and a new larger capacity sump that forced the return oil to travel around its perimeter for cooling prior to being picked up by the oil pump for re-use. Most of these improvements were only beneficial to the demanding owner, otherwise they lie in the 'nice to have' category as you would never know the difference in normal use.

Right up to the end of production constant development work was undertaken, with a variety of minor changes continually being made. The most significant was the introduction of the Zenith WIA42 carburettors at chassis 330498 (exception 330518) in lieu of the Stromberg DIV42 carburettors: this change resulted in a

Star Sapphire engine and Borg Warner type DG automatic gearbox prepared for display purposes, left. Cross section, below, reveals the hemispherical combustion chambers and inclined valves. Front view of the display unit shows the engine mounting. Five-bladed fan is home market specification, as are the wire type air cleaners.

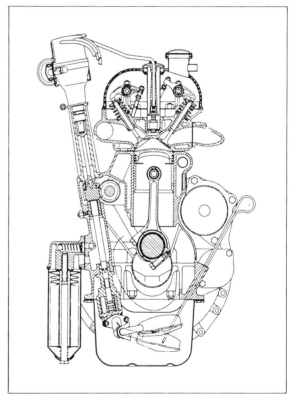

significant level of fuel saving of the order of 5mpg at normal operating speeds, but brought no saving at 100mph with only about 10mpg being possible at that speed in either case. At least one owner was known to complain about fuel consumption on a Star with the Stromberg carburettors and this car (330158) was then fitted with the later carburettors as a factory warranty cost. How many others were so dealt with is unknown but probably several as your author

157

knows of at least two other earlier Stars with the Zenith carburettors. Home delivered Stars had twin dry element air cleaners of the 'pot scrubber' type while export cars had similar air cleaners equipped with dry paper elements identical to those used on the P6 Rover V8.

The exhaust system for the Star was again designed in the traditional Armstrong Siddeley manner, but with a number of significant changes from the 346. The gases flowed from two identical manifolds down two front pipes through a Y-piece expansion box into a very large diameter intermediate pipe linking to a large and elaborate rear silencer, and from this silencer via a rear tailpipe (of ¼in larger diameter than the 346 pipe) to the rear, with a chrome plated angle cut embellisher for its end. The system provided better gas flow than the 346 system. The whole exhaust system was fabricated in heavy steel which was normal for the era. Stainless steel systems were virtually unknown then.

The first 174 cars (to chassis 330174) had their exhaust system mounted exactly as on the 346 with the now usual figure-8 hangers, rubber bushes etc. At chassis 330175 the whole hanging system was changed to the modern flexible laminated rubber strip hangers, to

158

provide more isolation from the chassis and thus less noise, though the improvement was a very marginal one.

The Star's radiator was identically mounted and was almost identical to the 346 radiator, excepting the header tank to water pump connection. The Star had the thermostat mounted on top of the water pump and thus the radiator top outlet was changed to a typical outlet flange rather than the earlier thermostat elbow cum outlet pipe. The cooling system was quite adequate in service so long as the radiator was kept clean which is essential for hot climate use.

When the Star limousine came out in 1960, there were yet another series of minor engine changes. Gone were the twin carburettors and instead the 346 type single manifold was reintroduced, together with a single downdraught WIA42 Zenith carburettor. This engine had a 140bhp rating. The other significant change was the introduction of four-point engine mountings in a similar front mounting arrangement to that used in the 234. The block was modified to provide a cast haunching to take this new mounting and special chassis mounts were developed also. This revised block casting can also be found on the last of the Star saloons, without the mounting system. It enabled far easier compressor installation when full air conditioning was specified.

There is little doubt that the factory saw the limousine as a formal car mainly for the hire-car trade, rather than as a driver's car, so they kept running and servicing costs down by offering a detuned engine. However, a keen owner could still specify twin carburettors, automatic gearbox, etc for his or her limousine if required.

The transmission

The Star Sapphire saloon was only offered with the British-built Borg Warner automatic gearbox, known as the DG series. This gearbox was very suitable for the Star and was also used on other heavy, high quality cars. It was a three-speed automatic with a variable second-speed ratio, and a vast improvement over the Rolls-Royce four-speed unit offered in the automatic 346 Sapphires.

This DG series gearbox was driven through a torque convertor which featured a direct-drive clutch for top gear lock-up. This avoided much of the typical automatic power wastage once top gear was in use – and this was most of the time. The larger level of engine torque ensured that the Star would mostly only need top gear for all but traffic work. These gearboxes are reasonably trouble free but early torque convertors gave some problems, mostly in the direct-drive clutch. However, the factory offered exchange units should any owner have problems, while today there are many specialist automatic gearbox reconditioners that are set up to overhaul these torque convertors as well as the gearbox, so owners should have no worry about service being available when required. The later torque convertors had improved clutch facings with greatly improved life, and these linings can be fitted to any convertor during a rebuild.

Interestingly, the concept of the direct-drive clutch within the torque convertor has been considered old fashioned technology for the last 20 years, but the new Japanese automatic gearboxes now coming into service in the mid 1980s have gone back to this concept

An extensively used publicity photo of the prototype Star Sapphire in final form as displayed at the Motor Show. The turned up front end of the chrome sill strip was a detail not adopted for the production version. This is the development car built on a 346 chassis, number C346925.

Two views of TDU 707, the 346-based development car, at an earlier stage, with some body details such as the mascot, bonnet central moulding, rear winkers and fog light position still to be finally decided.

160

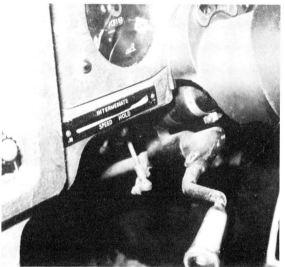

to ensure the overdrive ratio functions properly and fuel wastage in top gear is minimized.

The Star's gearbox controls included a cable operated variable second-gear hold; this was operated by a quadrant lever mounted on the instrument panel beside the switch cluster. This control was calibrated from 15 to 65mph and enabled the driver to choose the speed at which he wished to engage top gear. Once it was lifted above the 15mph setting, a first gear start was eliminated. Few owners ever bothered to move it from their chosen setting during normal usage.

When the Star limousine was introduced in early 1960 it was equipped with a four-speed synchromesh gearbox as standard, with the saloon's automatic gearbox being offered as an option – once again the preselective transmission was not offered. The actual build of the 77 long chassis worked out to be 64 with synchromesh gearboxes and 13 with the optional automatic.

The synchromesh gearbox was again purchased from Rootes Ltd and was the same gearbox that was fitted to the 346 saloons and limousines. However the actual change linkage was improved and

Details of the same Star Sapphire prototype, C346925, photographed during the early stages of restoration in 1985 in the garage at the original designer's home. Note the gearchange speed control mounted horizontally in the dash, and the four-point mounting, revised breather and new dipstick loction on the experimental engine, number EX97/12.

161

the four-point engine mount system helped too, so this gearbox installation became a joy to use.

The limousine synchromesh gearbox installation dictated a new steering wheel cowl and, in lieu of the window used for viewing the automatic selection, there was a raised plate which depicted the actual gear positions, while the gear-lever was very similar in appearance to the one on the automatic cars.

With the synchromesh gearbox installation in the standard limousine, a Borg and Beck 10in diameter clutch was used to couple the drive to the gearbox, and like the 234/6 Sapphires (but not the 346 Sapphires) was operated hydraulically. This added ease of control and a measure of lightness. The overall effect of these seemingly minor changes from the 346 installations was significant in operation and made driving the limousine far more fun than its predecessor.

The rear axle units for the Star were of the same family and basic type as for the late 346 Sapphires, once again the wonderfully reliable Salisbury brand, with the only significant difference being the ratios. The Star saloon had a 3.77:1 ratio (49/13 teeth), while the limousine ratio was 4.091:1 (45/11 teeth). It is interesting to note that the limousine used the same ratio as the 346 Saloon. The ratios chosen were the commonly available ones offered by the axle manufacturer, and the same crown wheel and pinion sets can also be found in a number of other cars such as Aston Martin, Jaguar and Daimler.

Wheels, tyres and hubcaps
Most items used on the Star models were the same as those used in the production of the earlier models, or minor variations thereof. The Star saloon used the same 16in Dunlop disc wheels as the 346 Sapphires up to chassis 330135 at which time the vent punchings were altered to permit better air flow, and this modification, of course, required alternative fittings for the dress rings. Visually these wheels are identical. The hubcap was the late 346 hubcap.

However, the Star limousine departed from tradition and introduced a 15in Dunlop disc wheel, which is superficially identical to the 234/6 wheel but has a ½in wider rim to accommodate larger tyres for a heavier car. Once again the hubcap is the same as was used on the 234/6 saloons and 346 limousines.

The advent of the radial tyre was just starting to make an impact on the motoring scene, amidst much prejudice. The ever conservative Armstrong Siddeley factory opted for standard cross-ply tyres from Dunlop for normal issue saloons and limousines, but listed a variety of alternative radial and high-performance cross-ply tyres as options. Most Star saloons came equipped with a soft riding but poor handling Dunlop 'Goldseal' style tyre. The saloon size was 670x16, while the limousine used a 760x15 tyre. An inspection of the old factory records for the Star saloon shows that the following tubeless alternatives were all used: Dunlop Goldseal with white walls; Michelin X (radials); Goodyear Standard four-ply; Goodyear 37 Nylon all-weather; Firestone standard; Firestone 500 Nylon; and Avon white walls. Tubed tyres also fitted by the factory were: Dunlop white walls; Firestone Town and Country; Michelin SDS; and Michelin X (radial). The Star limousines came equipped with 760x15 Dunlop tubeless tyres as standard and no mention can be found of factory-fitted alternatives in the old records.

Mechanical modifications

These changes are listed against a chassis number or, where appropriate, against the relevant engine number.

330051 Steering wheel cowl and shroud changed from painted cast alloy to black plastic – probably to eliminate poor appearance when paint became damaged.

330136 Road wheel ventilation slots modified on the inside – dress ring clips changed to suit.

330151 Heater and manifold water circulating pipe system changed back to the 346 system.

330176 Exhaust system hangers totally redesigned, replacing the traditional figure-8 hangers with the laminated rubber strip type.

320287 *(engine number)* Neoprene O-rings fitted to inlet valve guides to minimize oil loss into combustion chambers.

320451 *(engine number)* New distributor fitted with revised body and shaft bearing.

330501 New Lucas regulator control box fitted.

330501 Major revision to engine: **(a)** new larger cast alloy sump for better oil cooling; **(b)** larger water jacket (identified by long detachable side plates at top of righthand side of block); **(c)** dipstick repositioned; **(d)** new inlet manifold balance plug fitted; **(e)** revised pistons fitted with 'Britest' type scraper rings; **(f)** water pump body to manifold return pipe rerouted and repositioned; **(g)** new accelerator kick-down linkage and springs; **(h)** manifold changed to give additional clearance; **(i)** carburettors changed to Zenith WIA42 in lieu of Stromberg DIV42 (note this commenced at engine number 320506 excepting 320515).

330501 New style heavy duty tie-rod ends fitted (now the same as Daimler type DQ450); clamp lock on tie rods changed to lock nut system and different tie rods used.

330551 Engine exhaust downpipes slightly changed and heavier gauge exhaust pipes fitted.

330561 New rate front springs fitted to compensate for sagging after extended use.

320601 *(engine number)* Engine block changed in detail again with revised dipstick position, new rear thrust bearings – increased in number from two to four reverting to the 16/18hp practice. Haunchings added to front lower block (both sides) to take the four-point engine mountings only used on the limousine installations.

330661 Brake pedal slightly changed.

330751 Brake servo booster changed from Girling Mark 1 to Girling Mark 2 – many earlier cars now have the late booster or are fitted with PBR VH40 type boosters.

320801 *(engine number)* Timing chain cover changed – probably to allow for the belt drive on fully air-conditioned limousines and in readiness for the Mark 2 Saloon where air conditioning was to be offered.

330851 Slight change to stub axle.

Bodywork

Whilst the Star Sapphire's body at first glance looked very much like a 346 body, the eye was deceived as it was vastly different. As mentioned already most of the panels were different, changed for various reasons, and the whole finish and equipment was lifted to an extremely high level. Gone were the front opening front doors, the radiator grille was lowered and the bonnet line dropped significantly, while the nose of the bonnet was carried forward to cover the top of the grille in much the same way as the 18hp cars. The doors were shortened and a door step/sill introduced, which eliminated the dust and water problems the 346 cars experienced in some areas. A rear bumper bar apron (or gravel tray) similar to the 346 limousine was incorporated. More modern style bumper bars were fitted, the roof line at the rear was lowered and the rear quarter windows changed to suit, grilles were added where the fog lights had been to provide cooling for the disc brakes, the spats were cut away for easy tyre checking, and chrome strips were added to the waist line and the door sills. The traditional sphinx mascot was mounted on an elaborate bonnet feature (excepting cars for Swiss export). The overall effect of these changes was to make the car look longer and lower in general appearance, as well as more modern and faster than the 346.

With the exception of the changes to the radiator grille, the improvements were hailed by everyone as a big step forward; lots of people still feel the 346 radiator grille was better in appearance as the new grille was less imposing: I personally only feel this applies when viewing the car front on, as the side profile is more appealing to me with the new grille.

The Star's body was now thoroughly up to date, yet still very traditional, making it for many people an all-time classic. In service the body worked well and gave few problems, as most of the 346's minor irritations were eliminated in the redesign and upgrading. However, all this change introduced more areas for dirt and salt to accumulate with the inevitable rusting of bodies when used in

Star Sapphire bodies under construction in the Parkside factory on February 4, 1959. Production of the saloon version reached a final total of 902 cars.

unkind climatic conditions. This problem has caused the demise of a great many UK-delivered cars which would not have occurred had they been sold into dry climates. Out of the 902 saloons and 73 limousines it would seem that only about 40% remained in service after the first 25 years, mainly due to such a high proportion of production remaining in the UK where the winter operating conditions are so poor. That they fared so well mechanically, though, has encouraged people to restore the Star Sapphires that have survived, even though they are complex and far harder to restore than a 346.

Star Sapphire bodies are identified by having body numbers as follows: Star saloon, 35 plus four other digits (350001 to 350902); Star limousine, 36 plus four other digits (360001 to 360073). These body numbers appear in two places, being stamped on an elliptical plate mounted on the engine side of the bulkhead and also stamped into the inside face of the windscreen header rail on the lefthand side, but this latter marking is covered with trim when the car is complete. A restorer will find either the full body number or the last three digits written on the underside or inside of most bodywork items, as each car had an identifiable and specially matched set of trim and woodwork, and many panels were also identified in this way.

Like the 346, the Star Sapphire body was hand assembled and many items were especially fitted to each car. As the tolerances were close, the degree of individual fitting and adjustment was quite significant. The Star body has far fewer adjustable points than the 346; the door sill/steps were fixed as was the back of the front mudguard. This made the assembly far less flexible in execution and must have significantly added to production costs, being part of the price for a better finished body. However, the 346's step-by-step assembly concept remained excepting the front door to mudguard method.

Initially, when the body was fully assembled but not fitted out, it was painted and all underside areas, door interiors, and similar places were coated with a thick bituminous sound deadening material. Unfortunately this black protective coating was largely a failure, as it lifted off the surface and took the paint with it. This allowed water to attack the steel in many vulnerable parts, causing premature rusting. It did not take long to occur and the factory

The author's claims for the excellence of the Star Sapphire are based on 100,000 miles of practical experience: this is his 1959 model, chassis 330158, above, at close to 100mph and right, in repose.

1960 Star Sapphire, chassis 330841, a very late car finished in black over ivory paintwork, with matching black and ivory interior, a very stylish ensemble. Owner G. Harris.

corrected the procedure from about chassis 330500, reverting back to the 346 practice of applying the material (a different brand) to the panels only in sparing quantities, and generally not covering joints where movement would occur. It is largely for this reason that the later Stars are far less rustprone than the earlier ones.

The body was finished in nitrocellulose paint applied by hand, with much traditional hand rubbing between coats. The overall appearance was superb and many Stars still have original paintwork in good order to this day.

Once again the extensive chromium plating was not on to steel but rather on to brass or copper, excepting the bumper bars. This plating is of such high standard that most cars, even after nearly 30 years of exposure, still have this brightwork without much deterioration.

When the Star Sapphire was introduced there was an extensive range of new colours available as well as some of the old favourites. Like the 346 the cars could be ordered in single or two tone, but also a third variant was available, the painting of rear mudguards and spats in the same colour as the top of the main body. In these cases the mudguard piping was in top colour to ensure no visual break between panel and body.

Once the initial production runs were all sold, there was a significant demand for Stars with either special paintwork or, as some were sold by Rolls-Royce dealers, the Rolls-Royce special colour range was used for dealer orders. Thus the Star became the Armstrong Siddeley that had the greatest variety of colours ever available. New colours, exclusive for the Star, were Sand, Sable, Dark Grey, Light Grey, (both greys having a distinct blue tone), Green (apple), Ivory, Tan, plus Terra Cotta available later. Old colours available again were Black, Corinthian Green, Pearl Grey (as on the very late 346s), Cream, Sapphire Blue, Gazelle Fawn, Maroon, Elephant Grey and Silver Grey. Rolls-Royce colours, used on 22 cars, were Shell Grey, Tudor Grey, RR Sand, RR Sable, Steel Blue and Velvet Green. Special order colours that have been recorded are listed in Appendix 24.

The usable interior space of the body was slightly less roomy than before, due to the thickness of the seats and the angle of the back seat squab. The seats were all redesigned and were trimmed rather in the manner of the current Rolls Royce Silver Spirit, providing luxury for four rather than offering the compromise of regular six-seater

Interior trim of the Star Sapphire, with its split bench front seat upholstered in Connolly leather. Chassis number 330158. Seat belts are a non-standard addition.

167

1959 Star Sapphire engine compartment, showing later Zenith carburettors and export type air cleaners. Breather adaptation to satisfy later legal requirements is non-standard. Chassis 330158, engine 320169.

accommodation, though six people could be accommodated in reasonable comfort if required. The front seat was a split bench type in the now not unusual 40/60 configuration, later marketed by Buick as a new innovation. This 40/60 arrangement gives the driver a seat that is free to adjust to suit his or her needs, while the passenger's seat is extended and includes the central armrest and the extra width for the occasional central passenger. The seat cushions and squabs were upholstered in Connolly leather of the top quality 'Vaumol' range. This leather covering was fitted over specially shaped foam rubber mouldings, mounted on a spring base that was covered with a rubberized horse hair interface. The seats were thus of the highest quality and provided the maximum of support for fatigue-free travel.

The backs of the front seats were mostly fitted with a pull-out map pocket which was designed to take a street directory or thickish book. However, quite a few cars were delivered with picnic tables in lieu of map pockets. These tables still retained the visual appearance of the map pocket flap when not lowered for use. This was offered as a sales extra but not listed on the sales brochure. One Star (330706) even had a polished wood picnic table similar to a Rolls Royce Silver Cloud. The front seats were also available to special order with Reutter layback adjusters. The number of cars fitted with these extras is no longer available for research.

The door trims on the Star saloon were identical in general appearance to the 346 linings except that the shallow rear door pocket was eliminated, being considered unnecessary as this storage was replaced by the seat pockets. The armrests were slightly changed, the front ones now being vertically adjustable, while the rear side armrests were redesigned for better ingress and egress.

The vinyl on the side trims was carefully matched to the leather on the seats, so well that it is nearly impossible to detect which is which. The Star interiors were rather unusually colour co-ordinated, and the factory offered the following alternatives: **(a)** all trim the same colour; **(b)** all trim the same colour but seat piping and draught excluder velvet in contrasting colour, with the carpet often also

Star Sapphire tool kit, identical to that of later 346 cars. (Earlier 346 type had different oil gun.)

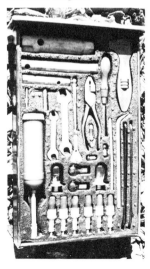

168

coloured to suit the piping rather than the seats; **(c)** trim in two-tone colourings, with light or contrasting centre panels in seats and door trims; **(d)** trim as preceding but also with piping to match the contrasting central panels, with the draught excluder and/or carpets often so matching as well.

The Star's interior leather colours were: Ivory VM 3323; Champagne (beige) VM3098; Red VM 3086; Grey VM3393; Green VM 3342; Tan VM 859; Blue VM 3015; and Blue VM 3500.

This extensive colour range, together with the use of two-tone colour schemes, produced some very stunning interiors, such as Tan with Champagne, Black with Ivory, Red with Ivory and so on. This, together with contrasting piping added even more flair. To some buyers of the 1959/60 era, this was all just too much and they reverted to ordering cars in simple single colour schemes with everything matching.

To complement this array of interior colour schemes, the factory produced the most magnificent sets of woodwork for these cars. The instrument panel was completely redesigned and made even more opulent than the 346 panel, while the rest of the woodwork followed exactly the same basic design, but was fully veneered in book-leaf matched burr walnut and all highly finished to the level used on a new grand piano.

In the case of the Star the headlining material could either be the now traditional ivory vinyl or alternatively a pale fawn or grey traditional English woven cloth material. In my view the cloth headlining looked altogether too drab. For the first time since the war the sun visors were recessed into the headlining and looked very tidy, even if less flexible in use, particularly in hot climates, as the new type could not be turned through 90 degrees to offer side-window protection.

The Star carpets were a new cloth and somewhat less velvet-like in appearance, having a distinct block pattern and grain. In all cases the Star's boot was also fully carpeted in the same material and all carpet was edged in self coloured cloth edging.

The interior door furniture was identical to the 234/6 models and was somewhat more traditional than the flamboyant thin handles and contrasting escutcheons used on the 346 models. The outside door handles were modernized to give a longer appearance than those previously used.

Minor improvements over the 346 introduced included new and entirely different door locks, giving a better closing action. The auxiliary lights were externally mounted, normally one fog and one driving light of the Lucas SFT576 and SLR576 type, on a stiffened front bumper apron.

At about chassis 330450 a script badge was fitted to the bootlid in the lefthand lower corner area and all dealers were instructed to fit these retrospectively to existing Stars, starting first with those in VIP use! Most Stars seem to have had these badges fitted in the warranty period.

An extensive list of body extras was offered: Webasto sun roof; radio with roof or crank-operated righthand telescopic aerial (HMV/Radiomobile brand seems to have been the preferred fitting);

For the Swiss market the prominent Star Sapphire bonnet mascot had to be replaced by this version, with the sphinx emblem in badge form rather than modelled, to meet legal requirements.

Reutter reclining front seat adjusters (assembly 2600013); picnic tables (assembly 2600104); laminated glass windscreen (standard in some markets); glove box lock (assembly 2600060); quick action window lifts (as fitted to 234/6); childproof door locks (assembly 2600089); special cold air ducts for USA and Canada (number 2512909); dipping mirror (number 2512791); flagstaff (number 251813); radiator blind (number 2512701); fitted suitcases; special cold air ducts for the Saudi Arabia market; special paint and colour schemes; wing mirrors; longer front seat slides (2in extra travel); and remote control door lock with garnish rails to suit.

During the course of the Star saloon production run, there were very few minor changes or modifications to the body. The changes which did occur happened at the following chassis numbers:

330250 (about) Deletion of central bonnet skin support from the hinge rail to eliminate the minor deflection of the bonnet line which sometimes showed up as a small dent.

330450 (about) 'Star' script badge fitted to boot lid during production.

330501 Lucas PL type headlights of 7in diameter now standardized. These were mounted in special step-down securing rims. Gone were the PL770's as used from the first 346. Cars for USA and Canada were always fitted with standard 7in sealed beam lights to satisfy their laws; cars for some other markets also had to meet different light requirements, and even different tail lights were fitted to some cars.

Limousine

The Star limousine was the last new car produced by the factory and, although a couple of pre-production cars were built in 1959, the limousine was essentially a 1960-only production run. In all there were 77 long or limousine chassis built, of which 73 had standard limousine bodywork, two of these being the pre-production cars.

The limousine body was essentially a combination of the Star saloon and the 346 limousine in concept, evolved like the saloon as a very much improved version of the preceding model. Externally the body was as might be expected of a stretched Star saloon except for a bulbous new bootlid with new fittings and furniture. This was introduced to give far better boot space and to allow room for the cool-air refrigeration plant which was boot mounted. The front doors, as on the saloon, were front hung, while the rear doors followed the 346 limousine practice and were rear hung which gave easy access for formal occasions.

The interior finish and appointments were largely new, with many significant changes over both the Star saloon and the 346 limousine which the new model replaced. The seats were somewhat altered, with the increased-width rear seat of the very late 346 limousine body retained, while the front seat squab was redesigned to offer a curved back support. The central division was also redesigned to give more leg room to occasional seat occupants, while

the open and fixed glass was rearranged. A new extra offered at a cost of £103 was an electrically dropped division and a few cars only were so equipped during production.

The biggest change came in the redesign of the polished woodwork and the various other trim pieces including all four door trims. The polished door cappings were narrowed, with a padded roll in trim material (leather or cloth) introduced along their lower edge. All door trims were completely changed and featured a padded, fluted top panel, and this treatment was also carried across the central part of the centre division, in the rear compartment. The rear seats had new side armrests and panels which incorporated Rolls-Royce style head pads on each side. Within these side trim panels were the controls for rear heaters, light, and, if fitted, air conditioning and electric drop division controls. The instrument panel was also modified and now incorporated a central ashtray (Whitley style) and for the first time a key-start ignition switch was used. The instruments themselves were also changed to an even more traditional style, being somewhat like an enlarged version of a Mark 1 346 Sapphire.

Imposing rear view of the Star Sapphire limousine. This is a 1960 production model, chassis 370009, owner J.A. Sloane. The bootlid shape was one of the details changed from the earlier 346 version.

Star Sapphire limousine instrument panel, on chassis 370009. Note the central ashtray in the style of the early 16hp, Whitley and 346 re-introduced for this model, and the key-start ignition switch.

Appointments of the rear compartment of the limousine. The central division and the polished woodwork were among the differences from the earlier model.

Limousine driving compartment. An electrically operated drop glass for the division in place of the sliding arrangement shown here was an option but was only fitted to a few cars.

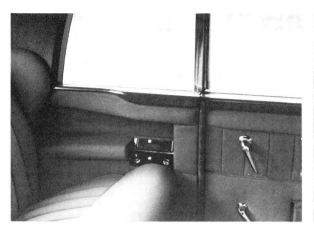

There were also other minor changes in equipment from the 346 limousine, including the standardization of quick action front door window lifts, snap pockets in the rear doors and the deletion of door pocket flaps on the front doors. All these appointment changes gave the Star limousine an entirely new, fresh and airy appearance.

For the first time ever the factory offered a full air conditioning installation as a standard option. This was based on the special system used for the Shah of Persia's 346 limousine and a handful of others. Air conditioned cars had modified bodywork at the front with two large side air intake grilles to ensure that the crossflow mounted condenser in front of the radiator would receive enough air flow. The four-point engine mount provided enough space for a swash plate type rotary compressor on the righthand side of the engine, while the main plant was housed in the boot immediately behind the rear squab. An air duct was introduced centrally below the rear window and the cold air was circulated into both the front and rear compartments via elliptical shaped glassfibre ducts, housed above the headlining. From these ducts there were four adjustable oblong vents. The control of this plant lay only with the rear seat occupants, from the side mounted controls previously mentioned.

Unfortunately there were very few customers for this elaborate and costly extra. However, the following cars were built and delivered with this system during production: chassis 40002 (factory demonstrator and pre-production car); chassis 370025 (sold in

More limousine interior details, including cloth upholstery and door trims for the rear compartment (left) and vinyl door trims in front (right).

Details of the controls fitted alongside the rear seats of a Star Sapphire limousine when air conditioning and an electric drop division were incorporated. Factory photographs of pre-production chassis 40002.

Details of the limousine boot-lid handle, number plate light and badge.

London); chassis 370040 (sent to Trinidad); chassis 370063 (sent to Hong Kong); and chassis 370064 (sent to Ghana). The quoted cost was almost £514 which added an extra 16% to the car's price – this was no doubt a very real disincentive to purchasers. At the time of writing the present whereabouts of these five cars is unknown. The pre-production car 40002 is understood to have been stolen from its owner in 1980 and has not been traced.

Although the brochure indicated that a large selection of paint colours were available, the cars built were actually finished in only a few of them, and, in keeping with the model's formal style, black was by far the most frequently requested, with 63 of the 73 standard limousines built being so painted. Of the remainder, there were two each in black and Dark Grey, black and Pearl Grey, and all-over Dark Grey; one each in Sand and Sable, Pearl Grey and Sable, and a special-order colour listed as Burgundy; and one car which escaped unrecorded. Available interior trim colours were brown, green, red, light blue, grey, ivory, black and beige.

The limousine was available with leather trimmed front seats and West of England cloth trim to the rear compartment. Mostly, the combination was black leather in the front with beige cloth in the rear compartment. However, all leather or matching cloth to leather was also available and several cars were so delivered. Even in a fully leather trim specification car the front door linings were still vinyl as on the 346 limousine – hardly worth the saving!

Three long-wheelbase Star Sapphire chassis were supplied to coachbuilders to be equipped as hearses: this retouched photo illustrates one such design.

The last four long or limousine chassis were supplied without bodies and delivery dates, coachbuilders and purpose were as follows: chassis 370074, July 1, 1960, built as a hearse by Windovers; chassis 370075, June 3, 1960 built as a hearse by Tilleys of Brighton; chassis 370076, May 27, 1960, a third hearse (coachbuilder unknown); and chassis 370077, May 6, 1960, built as an ambulance by Appleyards of Leeds.

The two Star limousines first displayed at the Motor Show were, in fact, the two pre-production or prototype cars used to develop the final production version, and they bore the special chassis numbers 40001 – registration number YDU 843 – and 40002 – registration number YHK 829.

Chassis 40001 was a standard limousine in all ways and was fitted with a synchromesh gearbox. The body was a rebuilt 346 body number 25/4/0382. This car was released from the experimental department for general use on December 31, 1959 with a mileage then of over 6,000. Chassis 40002 was an automatic gearbox limousine and featured all the factory options except the electric drop division. That item was subsequently fitted and, at the same time, the partition itself was repositioned. This car also had an experimental Star engine numbered EX/97/10 and was delivered to the sales department on December 1, 1959. Subsequent to the sale, the first owner outside the factory had picnic tables and occasional seats fitted, the order being dated July 27, 1960.

On the road

It had been said that the 16/18hp cars were outstanding town cars and reasonable highway cars, while the 346 Sapphire was a great highway car and a reasonable town car. The factory's goal was to make a great touring car also become a great town car and this is just where the Star fitted in.

As a town car, it was flexible, silky, very manoeuvrable, had a small turning circle and was very light to drive, while as a touring car it performed at least as well as the 346 Sapphire from which it evolved. There is no doubt that a Star could have been made faster by further engine tuning and have had more acceleration if a preselective or synchromesh gearbox had been employed. But these measures were never taken because the factory saw the Star as an elegant and graceful carriage rather than a sports car, and certainly it attracted most buyers in this category. To the best of the writer's knowledge, they have never been raced, hill climbed or rallied as they did not attract the motoring sport driver, but rather the business executive. The Star was one of that rare breed of cars that offer exceptional roadholding, cornering and riding, with high speed capabilities to match, yet when you come into town it changes its personality by becoming a graceful carriage. On the highway the cruising speed is determined by the driver with 80 to 90mph being a most relaxing gait. The cars are just able to exceed the 100mph mark and some examples have been known to have approached 110mph once run in and free. The acceleration is excellent from a standing start and particularly strong in the 50 to 80mph speed range.

When John Bolster tested the second Star (Chassis 330002) on June 26, 1959 for *Autosport* he recorded a standing quarter mile at 18.2 seconds which is still a respectable figure today and was then very quick for a heavy luxury saloon, and something many sports cars could barely achieve; he was also impressed with the way the acceleration surge went past 80mph and he covered many miles at 100mph. Having had several Stars I can well vouch for these comments.

Star facts

The first two production Star saloons were kept by the company as demonstrators: registration number WRW 442, chassis 330001; registration number WRW 910, chassis 330002.

The first Star produced for sale was chassis 330003 which was sold on December 8, 1958.

The earliest production Star sold was chassis 330004 which was delivered on November 10, 1958.

The last production Star sold was chassis 330902 which was sold on July 22, 1960 and exported to New Zealand where it is currently undergoing restoration in the hands of Rus Clement.

Armstrong Siddeley Managing Director (Mr Lindsay) ran the last car produced, 330873.

The last sale of a new Star on September 30, 1960 was chassis 330897.

No standard length Star chassis was fitted with a coachbuilt body.

Total of exported cars was 81 out of a production of 902 (about 9% of production).

Export sales by country:

Country		Country		Country	
Aden	1	Eire	8	Portugal	2
Australia	11	Ghana	1	Saudi Arabia	3
Belgium	2	Holland	2	Sierra Leone	1
Canada	6	Hong Kong	2	Switzerland	7
Canary Islands	1	India	2	Tanyanika	1
Cyprus	1	Japan	1	Trinidad	1
Denmark	1	New Zealand	20	USA	7

Prototype car (ex-346 chassis 346925) was registered TDU 707.

Star limousine prototypes were chassis 40001 and 40002.

The first Star limousine produced for sale was chassis 370003, delivered on February 12, 1960, and was also the earliest production limousine sold.

The last Star limousine produced for sale, chassis 370073, was delivered on October 21, 1960.

The last Star limousine delivered was chassis 370064, and was sold on November 26, 1960.

Original build sanction was for 75 production limousine chassis – all were built, numbered 370073 to 370077, this decision being confirmed by memo of February 19, 1960.

The last Star limousine chassis 370077, was bodied by Appleyards as an ambulance and not finished for delivery until January 1961.

6

Twilight

The Star Sapphire Mark 2, 1960

When the decision to stop car production was taken in early 1960 the experimental department were working on yet another stopgap, a revised or Mark 2 Star in saloon as well as convertible versions. One such car was actually produced using Star chassis 330905. What happened to chassis 330903 and 330904, the two missing numbers, remains a mystery; the frames may have been kept as spare parts, but nobody seems to know for certain, in spite of extensive inquiry. There was rumour of a second Mark 2 Star in the Bristol area but all trace has subsequently evaporated.

Let's look, therefore, at the only known Mark 2 Star. It is basically an amalgam of a Star saloon with lots of the special Star limousine features incorporated. Chassis 330905 was a standard length saloon chassis which was built to take the limousine's four-point engine mounting and the revised limousine rear spring mounting arrangements and repositioned differential. It is otherwise stock standard. The car is fitted with an experimental department four-point mounted engine, number EX/97/11, with twin Stromberg carburettors and revised breathing arrangements. It is coupled to the standard Borg Warner DG gearbox and standard Salisbury differential. The car runs on limousine 15in wheels with hubcaps and dress rings in limousine and 234/236 style.

The main variations are in the body. The car is fully air-conditioned with a plant of the type used in the limousine. The front mudguards were varied to incorporate slotted ventilation panels for the air conditioning condenser beside the grille and a four-headlight system was not very tastefully incorporated.

The scuttle ventilation panel was changed, with a fixed 'eyelid' cover, and the Star limousine bootlid was used. The rear window was enlarged into a semi-wraparound style, with the air conditioning intake vent situated immediately below it. Whilst the exterior changes were significant, it was the interior that underwent the biggest changes. The whole decor was modernized and its function significantly improved but at the cost of loss of the former classic appearance and, perhaps, also a loss of good taste. The seats were

When Armstrong Siddeley stopped producing cars, the experimental department had already developed a revised version of the Star Sapphire, intended as a stopgap until a genuinely new model was ready. The only surviving Star Sapphire Mark 2, and almost certainly the only one built, is chassis number 330905, seen here in 1985 as rescued for preservation by R. Cullingham. Main distinguishing features externally are the quadruple headlamps, the wraparound rear window and the raised bootlid borrowed from the Star limousine.

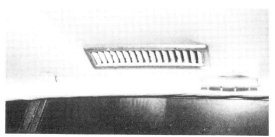

Star Sapphire Mark 2 details: revised scuttle ventilator and two of the air conditioning vents, an intake under the rear window and one of the cool air outlets in the rear passenger compartment.

fully redesigned and upholstered in large horizontal pleated panels with a contrasting top panel finely pleated. The front seats were an equally split bench with back rest adjustment by a conventional window lift handle set in the back corner. These seats each had Star saloon ashtrays set centrally in their back panels. The most impressive part is the quite extraordinary feature at the top of the squabs: the upper three or so inches converts firstly into a hinged headrest and then may be reversed to form twin picnic tables. This was an extremely ingenious piece of design that one would have thought would have been copied by other manufacturers. Both front seats had central armrests, as did the rear seat, and sliding adjustable armrests were fitted to the front doors as was usual Armstrong Siddeley practice. The rear seats followed the overall design and appearance of the front seats. New rear side armrests were incorporated into a padded corner cum headrest. These new seats do not look nearly as sumptuous as those of the normal Star but they are extremely comfortable.

The headlining was again the usual ivory nylon type, while the carpets were the conventional Armstrong Siddeley type, with very thick lambswool overlays. The door trims were similar to the Star limousine but the vertical pleated panels gave way to horizontal pleats to match the tops of the seat squabs. Quick action window lifts were fitted in the front doors. Around the edge of the roof and down the pillars the traditional woodwork was replaced with padded leather rolls, the grab handles were changed to full straps and on the top and bottom of the instrument panel was also a heavy padded roll, no doubt in the interests of safety at the price of beauty. Four seat belts were fitted, a first for Armstrong Siddeley. The Mark 2 had Star limousine style woodwork on the door cappings, but featured an entirely new instrument panel with large round adjustable air vents at each end. Star limousine instruments were installed and there was a complex central control panel with both slide and turn fresh

Front seating in the Mark 2
prototype, with prominent
transverse pleating and the
unique hinged top to each
seat which can be angled to
form a headrest or flipped
over, as shown right, to
reveal a picnic table.

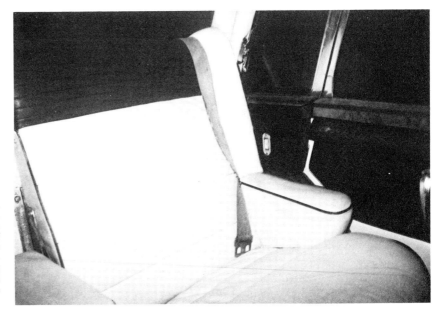

Rear seats in matching style,
with new armrests and
padded corners. The black
and white colour scheme of
this sole example adds to the
drama of the new decor –
what would Armstrong
Siddeley's clientele have
made of all this if it had gone
into production?

air and air-conditioning controls, a central mounted clock above a central radio and a row of toggle switches. The actual driving controls were identical to the Star saloon excepting the umbrella grip handbrake as used on the limousine and some export saloons.

The boot was conventional Armstrong Siddeley but its depth was restricted by the air-conditioning plant, the loss of space offset by the Star limousine bootlid. Alas, this was the last Armstrong Siddeley car manufactured. First registered on August 1, 1960, it was initially used by Sir Arnold Hall who was a highly distinguished chairman of the Hawker Siddeley Group and famous for his aerospace involvement. It was used within the Hawker Siddeley group until it was sold on August 7, 1966 at 72,419 miles. The car still exists and, as I write, it is undergoing some bodywork repairs.

The refined version of this car was to have been the stopgap model for two years until an all-new car was in production. On June 9, 1959 the proposal to build the car was put forward for board consideration: 'It is proposed that we introduce at the 1960 Motor Show a Mark 2 version of the Star saloon. Air conditioning will be available as an optional extra'. The papers depict the Mark 2 with single headlights and conventionally trimmed seats, which was certainly not the case with the only one produced. But whatever the details, the proposal was turned down. So chassis 330905 was the last Armstrong Siddeley car to leave the Parkside works after at least 52 years of car production. The factory still exists and is now part of the Rolls-Royce Aerospace division. It is used as a design centre and manufactures many classified products. Rolls-Royce Ltd (the aerospace company) is a 49% government owned trading company.

The car that never was
The Armstrong Siddeley factory design and development department were working on a replacement for the Sapphire and Star Sapphire range, originally projected for 1960 and later rescheduled for 1962, when the decision to cease car manufacture was implemented. From the same board meeting that considered the Star Mark 2 proposal, on June 9, 1959, comes the report, 'It is proposed that a new 4-litre saloon is developed for introduction during October 1962. The body is completely new. An improved Star Sapphire 4-litre engine, Borg Warner automatic transmission and front and rear suspension as Star Sapphire Mark II would be retained. Alternative power unit proposed is a V8 of $4\frac{1}{2}$ to 5-litre capacity. Proposed optional extras: air conditioning, electrically operated windows, reclining seats.'

They had employed Michelotti of Italy and had done several in-house design studies as well. Eventually they chose one of the latter in the form of a generous four-door saloon perhaps best described as something like a cross between a 3-litre P5 Rover and a Silver Shadow Rolls-Royce, with a very traditional radiator grille in a body recess somewhat like a Riley 4/72. The chosen design was created by a talented employee in the design office, Christopher Dunk.

The car was not to be of unitary construction, as that process was costed out and found to be inappropriate for small-volume manufacture at that time. So a widened, lowered chassis based on

Styling studies for the proposed new car, the development of which was never completed. They suggest a saloon of ample proportions and dignified mien. The frontal appearance seems to have been firmly established while a number of alternative tails were still under consideration, one in particular, the centre example in this group, revealing an Italian influence in its echoes of the Lancia Flaminia.

the Star Sapphire concept was designed to meet the requirements of strength, serviceability and acceptable cost. Most of this design work was completed in 1959 and they then made clay scale models, which, perhaps due to poor execution, did not seem to do justice to the design which was very modern and attractive. The next step was to do full sized wooden mock-ups, complete and sectioned. The factory also produced a body interior mock-up, and pictures of this during construction show a similar style to the 3-litre Rover of the era, especially the instrument cluster.

This car was to be offered with a choice of three engines: (1) a 2.7-litre four-cylinder engine, which was to be a reworked 234 engine with the 97mm bore etc (this option being a later addition to the range as originally proposed); (2) a 4-litre engine as used in the Star Sapphire Mk 2 prototype; (3) a 4.6-litre to 5-litre V8 with the now

Work on the new car progressed as far as a full-size wooden mock-up to establish details of the driving position, seating and interior trim.

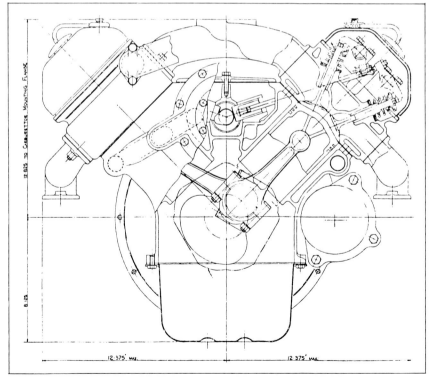

Cross-section of the new V8 engine with characteristic hemispherical combustion chambers and inclined valves very like those of the earlier in-line designs. Preparation for production of this power unit is believed to have reached an advanced stage when the project was cancelled.

usual Armstrong Siddeley crossflow head configuration. The factory planned to offer only the Borg Warner type DG gearbox, being the best automatic transmission then available.

It is believed that the experimental department had the V8 engine tooling well under way and that at least one prototype was produced. This prototype is believed to be still within the Hawker Siddeley family of companies, but your author has been unable to confirm this. If it exists, I feel it should be fitted to a car or at the very least kept in the Heritage Trust Museum at Parkside, where all can view it and contemplate what might have been.

I feel that the Star's replacement would have been a truly up-to-date carriage and would have pre-empted Rolls-Royce Motors by about four years: the Silver Shadow Rolls-Royce is a modern classic and I am sure the finished Armstrong Siddeley design would have looked equally beautiful and been highly successful in the context of the 1960s – alas it was not to be.

End of production

The board of Hawker Siddeley decided in March 1960 to cease car production on July 31, 1960. There are many views about this unhappy decision, but it would appear that there is not just one reason but there are several and it seems likely that it was a combination of facts that caused such a decision. I propose to set these out, and let my readers judge for themselves.

When the aviation and car interests of Armstrong Siddeley Motors and Bristol were merged in late 1959, the directors of Bristol gained greater say in the running of the newly merged car company, known as Bristol Siddeley Engines Ltd (still part of Hawker Siddeley at that time). They, it is said, did not like the prominence of the Armstrong Siddeley name and thought the Bristol name should reign supreme. It would seem that the group board of Hawker Siddeley had more major decisions to make and left the running of the Bristol Siddeley board to go its own way.

The Hawker Siddeley group, which owned Armstrong Siddeley Motors via the Bristol Siddeley Engines company, were preoccupied with advanced aero technology and manufacture. The Harrier, which was well under way, the engines for Concorde, and other projects, were all absorbing critical cash flow and requiring all available technical resources. The Star Sapphire was a stopgap in 1958, as funds for the Star's replacement for a 1962 scheduled release were witheld. Bristol Siddeley were in the forefront of aviation engines and specialist equipment manufacture and car production was relatively unimportant in the order of things. But the need for a new model was for 1958 or at the latest 1960, thus much impact was already lost.

The production capacity of the factory was contracted largely to Rootes Ltd, the staff having already designed the car that was to become known as the Sunbeam Alpine but was called internally the 'RAS' (Rootes Armstrong Siddeley). This major undertaking took the resources of Armstrong Siddeley Motors almost fully. It was a profitable and on-going contract in which they were freed of the costly involvement in marketing and back-up service, which were provided by the Rootes network. As it turned out only about two-thirds of the Alpine's production was built in the Armstrong Siddeley works, as it later became unprofitable to Bristol Siddeley Engines and Rootes took their manufacture elsewhere. However, the Alpine was a highly successful car that was largely developed by the Armstrong Siddeley staff – thus 'why make our own car in Coventry when we can make more money making someone else's car?'

The Star Sapphire Mark 2 was envisaged for release at the Motor Show late in 1960. This car was to be another stopgap until 1962 when the replacement would be ready. The costings put forward for this Mark 2 Star Sapphire were based on a 1,000 production run over the two year period. If 500 cars were produced in a year they estimated a loss of £70 per unit; however, if annual production were to reach 950 (a figure met and bettered in previous models) there would be a £57 pounds per unit profit – hardly anything to be excited about in 1960! One can well understand, when such figures were considered, why Armstrong Siddeley, such a minute part of the giant corporation, should have found their aspirations meeting with little approval from the group board.

The end of the Armstrong Siddeley car came on the last Friday in July 1960, when Star Sapphire 330905, the Mark 2 prototype, rolled out through the doors at Coventry.

On the Monday following, the accountants moved in with no soul and great force. There were one or two Mark 1 Star Sapphires still incomplete and they dictated that these were to be scrapped. These were probably numbered 330903 and 330904. They dumped most of the incomplete work, threw out panels that were considered to be in excess of likely demand, and so on. By the end of the first week in August 1960 all trace of Armstrong Siddeley car manufacture had gone.

One of the strange aspects of this production closure was that, after nearly 60 years of car production, the excellent staff still had not accepted the inevitable outcome of the board's decision, and on the fateful last Friday they were still working as usual, with no thought of the organisation ceasing manufacture.

In the months between the announcement of cessation of manufacture and the actual final build date, the demand for cars had continued at quite a pace. The factory also produced additional cars per week to enable a stockpile to be built up. These cars were moved from the Parkside Coventry factory to one of the group's aircraft facilities nearby at Anstey. The last car that was actually delivered to a dealer for sale was Star Sapphire limousine 370064 which was despatched to Ghana on November 26, 1960.

The board resolved to ensure that parts and service would remain available for at least 10 years, or however long they were required. They more than kept their word and spares were still available as late as 1971; modified parts were even still being designed and manufactured, service bulletins and dealer back-up continued.

In 1968, what had been Armstrong Siddeley Motors, now known as Bristol Siddeley Engines Ltd, was transferred to Rolls-Royce Ltd, with yet another name change to Bristol Engine Division of Rolls-Royce Ltd. This change did not at first in any way affect the arrangements for Armstrong Siddeley owners, but alas in mid-1971 Rolls-Royce Ltd crashed financially, and the receiver sold the spares and technical back-up to the Amstrong Siddeley Owners Club of the UK. The Australian Armstrong Siddeley Club also tried to buy the business, but their offer, although marginally higher, was rejected, as it was felt it should remain in England.

Incidentally, during the 1960s the board decided to sell the Bristol Car Company back to its founders and thus divested themselves of all car manufacture. The production of Sunbeam Alpines had already ceased after about 40,000 of the 60,000 production run were built. However, Humber Snipe engines continued to be built by Bristol Siddeley Engines.

Little did the board know in 1960 what they had given up. The name of Armstrong Siddeley is still known to most enthusiasts, with good examples of the marque fetching ever higher prices.

The service and spares supply was still outstanding, even though manufacture had ceased. The old established Armstrong Siddeley Motors spares department in Quinton Road, Coventry, was almost a legend, with the staff taking a personal interest in each car and its owner. The level of service right up until 1971 was way beyond the call of duty.

When the receiver for Rolls-Royce Ltd sold the Armstrong Siddeley spares and technical material to the English Owners Club, it was believed that the car manufacturing rights and the name also passed to the club. However, today this seems a little unclear. It may still be possible that the Hawker Siddeley group retained some of these rights when they sold Bristol Siddeley Engines Ltd to Rolls-Royce in 1968 so that these rights possibly never became part of the failed Rolls-Royce Company. In spite of investigation, your writer has never been able to prove this point either way, so I will leave it to someone else to unravel.

If Hawker Siddeley do own the car manufacturing rights, let's hope they will one day in the future see an opportunity to restart manufacture. The huge and highly successful Hawker Siddeley group are well able to organise such a venture. Whilst if the ASOC own these rights, their chances of recommencing manufacture must be very slim, no matter how willing the members are, as such a proposal would demand an astronomical amount of capital and knowhow. As the name is not lost, it is nice to contemplate a new Armstrong Siddeley car, but I feel the possibility of its coming into being is remote in the extreme.

The Armstrong Siddeley/Bristol Siddeley heritage is now being looked after by the Rolls-Royce Heritage Trust and they have established a museum at Parkside in the old factory with all manner of aircraft and car memorabilia. I was very heartened to learn in 1984/5 that the Star Sapphire 330873 that was used by Mr W.H. Lindsay, the last Armstrong Siddeley Motors managing director, is being restored for display. The museum also has the old boardroom furniture and corporation records back to the commencement of business.

7

Miscellany

One-offs and might-have-beens

Behind the scenes, the Armstrong Siddeley staff were almost always at work on possible new designs and the evaluation of proposed new models or new versions of existing ones. Many of these, of course, never progressed beyond the drawing board or mock-up stages, but during the postwar period a number of development cars and bodies were built. In keeping with company policy, few were ever sold to the public, most being kept for internal use and finally scrapped, and if detailed records were kept they have never become available for research. But a number of photographs, of cars, models and drawings, have survived and they tell an interesting story of constant development and of a very flexible approach to design. A selection of them are illustrated here to throw some more light on the way Armstrong Siddeley operated. Some of the designs were stepping-stones on the path to the cars that were put into production, some were not pursued but could well have been very successful had they been realized – others would have been disastrous!

The model in this photograph which dates from 1944 would appear to be a styling study for a full-width body on the 16hp chassis, and is more in the style of late prewar Continental designs than the English coachbuilt manner in which the cars were eventually to appear.

This body build during
latter part of World
Two, probably by Mull
Ltd, is being moved c
horse-drawn cart, pre
ably a wartime econc
The bulkhead is the ty
early postwar Armst
Siddeley shape.

The same body mounted on a
chassis in full running order,
with headlamp masks to
conform to wartime black-
out regulations and prewar
style radiator grille. This car
is presumably a progenitor
of the Lancaster.

Three photographs from 1945 of a pre-production Hurricane. Details which differ from the series production version include the cutaway rear mud-guards, triple door hinges, running board and front mudguard shape, large headlamps, chrome strips on the front bumper apron, rear bumperettes and tonneau cover. The wire wheels are the type offered as an extra on 16/18hp models.

This stylish drophead coupe is believed to be a 340 Sapphire prototype, captured by an unknown photographer outside the Armstrong Siddeley factory in mid 1950.

The Sapphire prototype, often referred to in factory documents as the 340 Sapphire. Details to note are the hidden centre pillar, fabricated bumpers, 16/18hp style mascot, door handles, locks and trim panels, hubcaps, plain interior, and the shape of the rear quarter window, all of which were to be changed before production. This car may well have been fitted with the W.O. Bentley designed twin-cam engine.

Boot arrangement of the 340 Sapphire prototype, with boxes to check its capacity.

Styling study for the front end of the Sapphire: this one was almost certainly never more than a sketch.

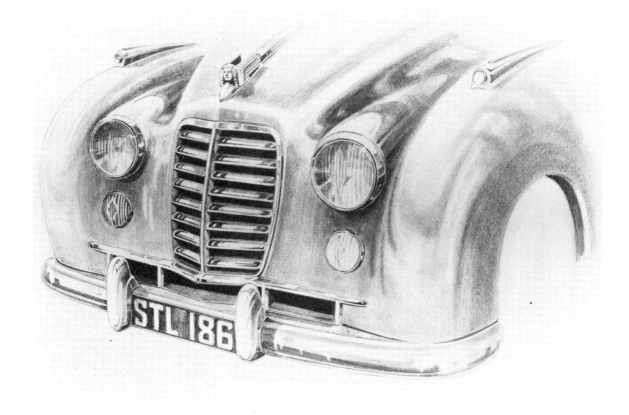

Above: very little is known about this mystery car. It would appear to be complete, not just a mock-up, and Armstrong Siddeley factory drawing number 188000 indicates that it was an alternative body for the 234 chassis. The style closely resembles Pinin Farina designs of the period, but its origins are not confirmed.

Above left: the 234 prototype on test. Sloping tail and front end were later altered. Left, another rear-end treatment, on an early pre-production 234 or 236 Sapphire.

193

Boot layout and rear lights of the early pre-production 234/236.

A late pre-production 234 Sapphire, as photographed for the sales brochure. Humber side grilles and winkers were changed later, and separate parking lights and badges have yet to be added.

More shots of the pre-production 'Baby Sapphire', very close to the definitive version but with details like the rear lights, rear window shape and petrol filler still to be finally settled.

Styling studies for the
excellent 234/236 chassis.
Above, a sketch dated
September 1958 for what
could have been a Mark 2
version. Right, a clay model
for a saloon in the 'fastback'
manner, again post-dating
production, and below, a
stylized rendering of an open
car of advanced design.
There is no evidence that any
of these progressed any
further, more's the pity.

196

The Sphinx sports racer

The Sopwith family had long been involved in the management of the Armstrong Siddeley factory and other corporate ventures, and in the 1953-54 period the factory produced a hybrid sports-racing car which made its debut at Goodwood on March 27, 1954, Tom Sopwith the younger being both the instigator of the design and the driver of the finished car.

The Sphinx, as it was called, was modelled on other sports-racing designs of the era, and had a likeness to the DB3S Aston Martin, with a front not unlike the original Testa Rossa Ferrari. Developed and produced within the Armstrong Siddeley works, the car had an Allard JR chassis with de Dion rear suspension.

The engine was a worked-over 346 Sapphire unit with the standard 90mm bore and stroke: it had strengthened crankshaft, special high-lift camshaft, triple double throat Weber carburettors and an extractor exhaust system with six large pipes from the head. I am told the engine developed 227bhp on 100 octane fuel running a 9.5:1 compression ratio.

This engine drove the traditional 346 Sapphire preselective gearbox with standard electric control. The differential ratio is quoted as 3.55:1 but was probably changed to suit each racing circuit. The wheels were 16in wire knock-off type, with 600x16

Top, another version of the 234/236 proposal for 1959: how well would this dream-car style have translated into reality? Above, the Star Convertible design, at one stage scheduled for release in late 1960 as part of the Star Sapphire Mark 2 project, but never produced.

197

Dunlop racing tyres being fitted.

The dramatic and purpose-ful looking Sphinx sports-racing car, built by Armstrong Siddeley for Tommy Sopwith to race under the Equipe Endeav-our banner. Based on an Allard chassis, it was 346-powered.

Experience with this project may well have contributed to the engine development work which led to both the Star Sapphire power unit and the related four-cylinder 234 version, but a full-scale racing programme was hardly Armstrong Siddeley's style and the factory were very half-hearted in their support. It was a period too when the rate of technical progress in sports-car racing was speeding up, with major efforts being mounted by manufacturers like Aston Martin, Jaguar and Mercedes-Benz. In consequence, the Sphinx soon faded from the scene, and Sopwith's team, *Equipe Endeavour*, went on to achieve considerable success racing, ironically enough, Jaguar saloons.

About the author: a passion for Armstrong Siddeleys

Armstrong Siddeleys have been a passionate interest of mine since before I was a teenager. During the war my father had a 1934 Fifteen saloon, chassis 67291, which he kept until 1948, and it was the first car I can remember. The family association with the marque goes back further still, to 1932, when my grandfather bought a Twelve saloon with a Cresswell body built in Sydney. In more recent years both my sons have purchased 346 Sapphires and my daughter hopes to buy one when she is old enough to drive.

My first car was a 1934 Twelve saloon (chassis 91020) which I proudly purchased on June 6, 1956, when I was just 19. It arrived as a non-runner, semi-dismantled, in a pantechnicon, and getting it on the road again gave me a huge task and taught me many skills. Over the three decades since that first Armstrong Siddeley, I have owned and used every basic postwar model including examples of every body style except the limousine versions of the 18hp and the Star Sapphire, neither of which have ever come to Australia – a situation I plan to remedy one day! The list also includes a 1925 Short Eighteen Mk2 and a 1936 Twelve Plus, and currently I have a superb 1935 Siddeley Special to keep several postwar models company.

Cockpit and dashboard of the Sphinx, including the Sapphire-style control for the preselective gearbox, a type of transmission which was also used in other racing cars including ERA and Connaught.

My Armstrong Siddeley activities have always turned out to be complex and diverse. Re-framing the body of my original Twelve is a lasting memory. Subsequently I have completed full restorations of a Lancaster, a Whitley, several 346 saloons, a 346 limousine, a 236 Sapphire and two Star Sapphire saloons. I have also done all the maintenance and repair work required on all the Armstrong Siddeleys I have owned, including mechanical rebuilds, body work and much interior retrimming, always striving to get as close as possible to the perfect job. It has been a sort of duty to the cars rather than any kind of profit orientated activity. The current project at the time of writing is the restoration of a 346 Sapphire (chassis 340075) which has the third four-light body built and was the first four-light Sapphire sold new to the public, the first and second cars having been retained as factory demonstrators.

In 1949 I started writing to the factory and since that date I have kept every letter or piece of information that has come my way. In the period after the end of production until the Rolls-Royce takover in 1968, and then on until the 1971 collapse of Rolls-Royce, I constantly probed for additional data and material, much of which was supplied by the ever willing former Armstrong Siddeley Motors staff. In this way I gradually accumulated a huge resource which has combined with the practical knowledge gained from working on the cars to provide the basis for this book. I have tried to make the book not only a readable history and a reference work for the browser but also one that will guide restorers in areas of authenticity and originality beyond what is provided in the usual technical manuals and handbooks.

My employment has been completely separate from cars, centred around valuation, real estate and property development. I have also run my own retail store and managed a building society office. Since 1982 I have been a full-time teacher of real estate and valuation subjects in the School of Business Studies at Canberra TAFE College. Thus the car interest has always remained a hobby, a labour of love and something I have never tired of. Working in an office environment all day, I find it essential to use my hands at weekends, and the ever-satisfying activity of car restoring provides the ideal recreation.

Altogether, my wife and I have owned about 40 Armstrong Siddeleys, and our total mileage in them now exceeds 750,000, but we have also found time to be owners of other English makes, and have enjoyed Aston Martin, Lagonda, Rolls-Royce, Bentley, Daimler, Jaguar, MG and Jensen cars. They all have good qualities but I still find the Armstrong Siddeley to be the best all-round car for a whole series of reasons, some of which I hope have already emerged in my account of their development and production. Above all, the Armstrong Siddeley is a car of great character, one that becomes part of the family, never just a purely utilitarian machine. Its style, mechanical excellence, high quality detail finish, ruggedness, ease of maintenance and long-term economy are all part of the appeal.

But perhaps the pre-eminent quality is the effortless way all the models have been able to cope with long journeys, leaving driver and passengers remarkably fatigue-free, something particularly appreciated in a country of long distances like Australia. During the late 1970s I lived in Armidale NSW and had cause to make frequent business trips to Melbourne some 900 miles distant. I used to leave at about 6am, be in Narrandera, 500 miles away, for lunch, and arrive in Melbourne for the end of the rush hour at about 7pm. I used a Sapphire (chassis 340426), a 1953 model with single carburettor and preselective gearbox, converted into a utility: it had already done over 400,000 miles when these trips became a more or less regular occurrence, and it never once let me down.

My 234 (chassis 4230454) provided some particularly memorable journeys. Accompanied by my wife, two young children and a seven-month-old baby, I drove to an ASCC rally in Swan Hill, Victoria, from Sydney where we then lived, a distance of 620 miles. We felt that 450 miles in a day was enough with a young baby and consequently booked into a motel at Hay which was about the right distance. Leaving home shortly after dawn, we arrived in Hay for a 1.30pm lunch, and so had an afternoon to fill in a very small town! The next morning we again left at about dawn and revelled in the open countryside, letting the 234 have its head and covering the remaining 170 miles in only about two hours which was rather naughty, so that we arrived in Swan Hill for breakfast. After the rally we toured on to Adelaide and came back to Sydney via Melbourne, covering over 3,500 miles in our nine-day break. I am glad to say that this car is still in as-new condition, as Pauline Elliott, to whom we sold it, is a most fastidious owner and maintains it superbly – it may well be the best 234 in the world.

At least 100,000 of my Armstrong Siddeley miles have been in Star Sapphires, in my opinion the greatest model of them all. The Star's ability to cover huge distances has been well proven in the Australian outback. One day in 1979 I motored from Adelaide in South Australia to Armidale in northern NSW, a distance of 1,177 miles, in Star 330382, with my wife, three children and a boot full of luggage. The journey took 17 hours and 10 minutes, including an hour for lunch at Broken Hill, about an hour and a half at Nyngan for dinner, and numerous petrol and comfort stops. Arriving home just after midnight, we were all very tired but I could have gone on another 300 miles to Brisbane had it been essential. We covered the 500 miles of desert at a steady 100mph with no complaints from the Star at all. Routine fluid level checks were all that was required – though petrol consumption at 100mph was only slightly in excess of 10mpg. At that time the car was 20 years old and had done over 125,000 miles! That car too is still in outstanding condition and is now also in the Elliott collection.

I consider the Armstrong Siddeley to be one of the all-time great cars: I have never been able to understand why it has so often been underrated, often by people who sit in judgement without ever having owned one. Talk to an Armstrong Siddeley owner and you will soon find how deep is the genuine attachment. My involvement with the cars has made me friends with thousands of people not only in Australia but in several other countries, as the fellowship among the owners of the marque is so strong, opening most doors and crossing all social, economic and racial barriers.

The Armstrong Siddeley Car Clubs

This deep commitment to the marque led a group of us in 1958/9 to investigate the feasibility of starting an owners' club in Australia. One-make clubs were comparatively rare at that time, as the thriving motoring movement of today was only in its infancy. However, in 1960 some seven enthusiasts formalized the Australian Armstrong Siddeley Car Club, with your author as its first president and vehicle historian. It was the first Armstrong Siddeley club in the world and the only one to be in existence before the company stopped manufacturing cars. Shortly afterwards the Armstrong Siddeley Owners Club in the UK made a tentative start, being reformed in 1966. In 1970 came the New Zealand club, and in more recent years clubs have sprung up in the Netherlands, Switzerland, the USA and Finland. As I write there are moves afoot to formalize into a structured club the loose-knit band of owners in Venezuela. A new club in Japan is a recent possibility too.

Three generations of post-war Armstrong Siddeley at a gathering of the Australian ASCC. The fellowship of owners is well established in a number of countries round the world, as befits a marque that was widely exported in its heyday.

These clubs look after a large number of owners around the world; the numbers are increasing all the time and further new clubs will no doubt be formed. Out of them has sprung an extraordinary worldwide fellowship of owners dedicated to the restoration, preservation and enjoyment of Armstrong Siddeley cars and their predecessors. The cars were extensively exported, to at least 70 countries over their 41 years of manufacture, and this spread has been continued by owners taking their prized examples with them as they moved to other countries. In more recent years cars from England have been acquired by enthusiasts overseas, particularly in the USA and the Netherlands. Thus cars are now often located thousands of miles from their point of original sale.

The Armstrong Siddeley clubs provide technical back-up and often a parts pool for their members, and most clubs keep historical records of all the cars in their area. This mutual sharing of information and assistance makes the major tasks of rebuilding and restoring both rewarding and enjoyable. The social aspect of the clubs draws together people from many regions and from all walks of life. If you own an Armstrong Siddeley, or are an enthusiast of the marque, membership of your nearest club is a must, ensuring you a whole new set of friends and a continuing and developing interest.

8

Appendices

Appendix 1
16hp engine specification
Cylinders	6
Bore	65mm/2.559in
Stroke	100mm/3.937in
Capacity	1,991cc
Compression ratio	7:1
Carburettor	Stromberg
Max power	70bhp at 4,200rpm
Max torque	96lb/ft at 2,500rpm
RAC rating	15.72hp (nominal 16hp)

Appendix 2
18hp engine specification
Cylinders	6
Bore	70mm/2.756in
Stroke	100mm/3.937in
Capacity	2,309cc
Compression ratio	6.5:1
Carburettor	Stromberg
Max power	75bhp at 4,200rpm
Max torque	108lb/ft at 2,500rpm
RAC rating	18.22hp (nominal 18hp)

Appendix 3
16/18hp gearbox ratios
	Synchromesh	Preselective
Fourth	1:1	1:1
Third	1.419:1	1.416:1
Second	2.135:1	2.09:1
First	3.452:1	3.6:1
Reverse	2.982:1	4.469:1

Standard final drive ratio 5.1:1

Appendix 4
16/18hp models: dimensions
Standard models
Wheelbase 9ft 7in, front track 4ft 6in, rear track 4ft 6½in, width 5ft 8in, turning circle 37ft, kerb weight approx 29-30cwt (Utilities 28cwt). Length: Hurricane 15ft 6in, Lancaster 15ft 7½in, Typhoon 15ft 6in, Whitley 15ft 5in, Utilities 15ft 5in.

Limousine
Wheelbase 10ft 2in, front track 4ft 6⅝in, rear track 4ft 9in, width 5ft 10in, turning circle 38ft, kerb weight approx 35cwt, length 16ft 3in.

Appendix 5
16/18hp chassis production data
Batch	Chassis numbers	Production
ZG	160001 to 160045	45
ZH	161001 to 162000	1,000
ZJ	162001 to 163000	1,000
ZK	163001 to 164000	1,000
ZL	164001 to 165000	1,000
ZM	165001 to 166000	1,000
ZN	16/186001 to 16/187000*	1,000
ZO	16/187001 to 167156/188000*	1,000
ZP	188001 to 188500	500
ZR	188501 to 189500	1,000
ZS	189501 to 1810650	1,150
ZT	1810651 to 1811150	500
ZU	1811151 to 1811800	650
ZW	1811801 to 1812450	650
ZX	1812451 to 1813300	850
Total (standard chassis)		12,345
Long chassis:		
First batch	18001 to 18100	100
Second batch	18101 to 18125	25
Total (long chassis)		125
Total, all 16/18hp cars (excluding prototypes)		12,470

Batches ZN and ZO were built during the changeover from the 16hp engine to the 18hp: the basic four-figure chassis numbers ran sequentially through each batch of 1,000, with the prefix 16 or 18 applied to each individual chassis according to which engine was to be fitted. Last 16hp chassis was 167156.

Appendix 6
16/18hp body production data

Body numbers	Body type	Production
1 to 500	*not allocated*	
501 to 999	Hurricane	499
1000	Typhoon	1
1001 to 2000	Hurricane	1000
2001 to 3700	Typhoon	1700
3701 to 4000	*not allocated*	
4001 to 4700	Hurricane	700
4701 to 6000	*not allocated*	
6001 to 8500	Lancaster	2500
8501 to 8577	Utility Coupe	77
8578 to 8700	Station Coupe	123
8701 to 8790	Utility Coupe	90
8791 to 8875	*not allocated*	
8876 to 9000	Lancaster	125
9001 to 9006	'Tempest'	6
9007 to 9025	*not allocated*	
9026 to 9300	Lancaster	275
9301 to 9800	Whitley	500
9801 to 9950	Utility Coupe	150
9951 to 10100	Station Coupe	150
10101 to 10250	Utility Coupe	150
10251 to 10400	Station Coupe	150
10401 to 10500	Lancaster	100
10501 to 10600	Limousine	100
10601 to 10715	Utility Coupe	115
10716 to 11000	Station Coupe	285
11001 to 11300	Lancaster	300
11301 to 11464	Hurricane	164
11465 to 11500	*not allocated*	
11501 to 11750	Whitley	250
11751 to 12000	Station Coupe	250
12001 to 12710	Whitley	710
12711 to 12900	Station Coupe	190
12901 to 13000	Lancaster	100
13001 to 13135	Utility Coupe	135
13136 to 13159	Limousine	24
13160	Lancaster	1
13161 to 13590	Whitley	430
13591 to 13824	Hurricane	234
13825	Typhoon	1
13826 to 13834	Hurricane	9
13835 to 14000	*not allocated*	
14001 to 14070	Station Coupe	70
14071 to 14250	*not allocated*	
14251 to 14560	Whitley	310
14561 to 14839	Whitley six-light	279
14840 to 14869	*not allocated*	
14870 to 14972	Whitley	103
Total, standard types		12,356

Production totals, standard bodies

Hurricane	2,606
Lancaster	3,597
Utility Coupe	717
Station Coupe	1,022
Typhoon	1,701
Whitley	2,303
Whitley six-light	279
Limousine	122

There were additionally 112 chassis delivered to various independent coachbuilders, one used by the factory experimental department (probably to test the Sapphire engine) and one fitted with a station wagon body : these 114 complete the total of 12,470 chassis known to have been produced. For an explanation of the provenance and accuracy of these figures, see page 45.

Notes:

Typhoon: *single early Typhoon (1000) was a factory-converted Hurricane; single late car (13825) was assembled with metal roof to special order.*

'Tempest': *title used for six cars (9001 to 9006), in effect four-door Typhoons, which prefigured Whitley production.*

Whitley: *body 9796 factory converted from four to six-light.*

Limousine: *bodies 10568 and 13147 factory converted to landaulette.*

Hurricane: *bodies from 13591 onwards with Whitley-style tail.*

Appendix 7
Non-standard 18hp engine numbers

There were 29 engines in the 18hp series identified by numbers outside the normal engine numbering sequence. The reason for this has not been recorded – possibly they were a pre-production run – and they were not apparently different in construction: a note on the original list suggests that an attempt was made to correct the numbers. The first of these engines, 180001, was probably used for testing but the other 28 were fitted to chassis in normal production, though out of sequence and with normally numbered 16hp and 18hp engines interposed between them.

Engine number	Chassis number	Chassis number	Engine number
180002	186466	186157	180004
180003	186160	186158	180028
180004	186157	186159	180013*
180005	186282	186160	180003
180006	186258	186165	180012
180007	186271	186166	180015
180008*	186175	186175	180008*
180009	186260	186176	180029
180010	186179	186178	180022
180011	186280	186179	180010
180012	186165	186232	180017
180013*	186159	186249	180016
180014	186261	186258	180006
180015	186166	186259	180018
180016	186249	186260	180009
180017	186232	186261	180014
180018	186259	186266	180027
180019	186287	186271	180007
180020	186283	186280	180011
180021	186284	186282	180005
180022	186178	186283	180020
180023	186371	186284	180021
180024	186290	186287	180019
180025	186291	186290	180024
180026	186323	186291	180025
180027	186266	186323	180026
180028	186158	186371	180023
180029	186176	186466	180002

The factory record accommpanying this data notes: 'Two engines E180013 and E180008 have already been renumbered E186013 and E186008 and these two numbers will remain, as they have been supplied to the Customs Authorities, but special note must be kept.'

Appendix 8
Sapphire 346 engine specification

Cylinders	6
Bore	90mm/3.543in
Stroke	90mm/3.543in
Capacity	3,435cc
Compression ratio:	
Most cars*	7:1
Pick-up	6.5:1
Carburettor/s	Single or twin Stromberg
Max power:	
Early cars	120bhp at 4,200rpm
Single carb	125bhp at 4,400rpm
Twin carb	150bhp at 5,000rpm
Pick-up	100bhp
Max torque:	
Single carb	182lb/ft at 2,000rpm
Twin carb	194lb/ft at 2,000rpm
Pick-up	160lb/ft at 2,000rpm
RAC rating	30.13hp (nominal 30hp)

some variation, see text

Appendix 9
Sapphire 346 gearbox ratios

	Synchromesh	Preselective	Automatic
Fourth	1:1	1:1	1:1
Third	1.42:1	1.36:1	1.45:1
Second	2.09:1	1.993:1	2.634:1
First	3.13:1	3.4:1	3.82:1
Reverse	3.31:1	4.76:1	4.304:1

Standard final drive ratio 4.091:1
Limousine final drive ratio 4.451:1

Appendix 10
Sapphire 346 dimensions

Saloon
Wheelbase 9ft 6in, front track 4ft 8⁵⁄₈in, rear track 4ft 9¹⁄₂in, width 6ft, length 16ft 1in, turning circle 42ft, kerb weight approx 32¹⁄₂cwt.

Limousine
Wheelbase 11ft 1in, front track 4ft 9⁵⁄₈in, rear track 5ft 0⁵⁄₁₆in, width 5ft 11¹⁄₂in, length 17ft 8in, turning circle 42ft 6in, kerb weight approx 36cwt.

Pick-up
Wheelbase 9ft 6in, front track 4ft 9⁵⁄₈in, rear track 5ft 0⁵⁄₁₆in, width 6ft, length 15ft 7¹⁄₂in, turning circle 43ft, kerb weight approx 37cwt.

Appendix 11
Sapphire 346 production data

Batch	Chassis number	Production
A	340001 to 340050	50
B	340051 to 340250	200
C	340251 to 340500	250
D	340501 to 340750	250
E	340751 to 341000	250
F	341001 to 341250	250
G	341251 to 341500	250
H	341501 to 341750	250
J	341751 to 342000	250
K	342001 to 342250	250
L	342251 to 342500	250
M	342501 to 342750	250
N	342751 to 343000	250
O	343001 to 343250	250
P	343251 to 343500	250
R	343501 to 343750	250
	end of Mark 1 production	
S	343751 to 344000	250
T	344001 to 344250	250
U	344251 to 344500	250
V	344501 to 344750	250
W	344751 to 345000	250
X	345001 to 345250	250
Y	345251 to 345500	250
Z	345501 to 345750	250
AA	345751 to 346000	250
BA	346001 to 346250	250
CA	346251 to 346500	250
DA	346501 to 346750	250
EA	346751 to 347000	250
FA	347001 to 347250	250
GA	347251 to 347297	47
–	347298 to 347697	400

Appendix 12
Sapphire 346: cars assembled in Belgium
Chassis numbers

340447	340448	340449	340450	340451
340735	340736	340737	340738	340739
340882	340883	340884	340885	340887
341081	341082	341083	341084	341086
341183	341184	341185	341186	341187
341188	341315	341316	341317	341318
341319	341320	341530	341531	341532
341533	341534	341535	341536	341751
341752	341753	341754	341755	341756

(plus four other numbers not recorded)

Appendix 13
Sapphire 346: oil company pick-ups
Chassis numbers

346930	346931	346933	346934	346935
346936	346937	346938	346939	346940
346941	346942	346943	346944	346945
346946	346949	346952	346958	346973
346979	346981	346990	346993	346995
346996	346997	346998	346999	347000
347084	347093	347095	347113	347114
347116	347117	347118	347133	347134
347141	347146	347184	347188	347189*

*Only example to remain in UK, only known survivor

Appendix 14
Sapphire 346: Vincent limousines

Chassis number	Engine number	Body number	Delivery date	Registration number	User's name
EXL/340/13	EXP/340/10	L25/3/001	27/2/53	MVC 123	Sir Frank Spriggs
EXLC/340/2	E340009	L25/3/002	19/2/54	OWK 862	Mr Crabbe Gloster Aircraft Co
EXLC/340/3	E340024	L25/3/003	1/9/53	ODU 920	Mr Woodhams Armstrong Whitworth Aircraft Co
EXLC/340/4	E340102	L25/3/004	1/9/53	ODU 924	Sir R. Dobson Avro Aircraft
EXLC/340/5	E340219	L25/3/005	–	–	N. Spriggs Hawker Aircraft (Kingston)

Appendix 15
Sapphire 234 engine specification

Cylinders	4
Bore	90mm/3.543in
Stroke	90mm/3.543in
Capacity	2,290cc
Compression ratio	7.5:1
Carburettors	Twin SU
Max power	120bhp at 5,000rpm
Max torque	140lb/ft at 3,500rpm
RAC rating	20.09hp (nominal 20hp)

Appendix 16
Sapphire 236 engine specification

Cylinders	6
Bore	70mm/2.756in
Stroke	100mm/3.937in
Capacity	2,309cc
Compression ratio	7.5:1
Carburettor	Stromberg
Max power	85bhp at 4,400rpm
Max torque	117lb/ft at 1,750rpm
RAC rating	18.22hp (nominal 18hp)

Appendix 17
Sapphire 234/6 gearbox ratios
Fourth 1:1   First 3.452:1
Third 1.419:1   Reverse 2.982:1
Second 2.135:1   Overdrive 0.778:1
Standard final drive ratio 4.545:1

Road speed and engine rpm

Gear		O/D fourth	Fourth	O/D third	Third	Second	First
Overall ratio		3.536:1	4.545:1	5.108:1	6.450:1	9.703:1	15.692:1
MPH	KPH						
10	16	458	588	648	834	1,254	2,028
20	32	916	1,176	1,296	1,668	2,508	4,056
30	48	1,374	1,764	1,944	2,502	3,762	6,084
40	64	1,832	2,352	2,592	3,336	5,016	
50	80	2,290	2,940	3,240	4,170	6,270	
60	96	2,748	3,528	3,888	5,004		
70	112	3,206	4,116	4,536	5,838		
80	128	3,664	4,704	5,184			
90	145	4,122	5,292	5,832			
100	160	4,580	5,880				
110	176	5,038					

(Dunlop 640 x 15 tyres, effective rolling diameter at 30mph = 26in or 775 revs per mile)

Appendix 18
Sapphire 234/6 dimensions
Wheelbase 9ft 3in, front track 4ft 7$\frac{1}{8}$in, rear track 4ft 6$\frac{5}{16}$in, width 5ft 8$\frac{1}{2}$in, length 15ft, turning circle 40ft, kerb weight approx 27cwt.

Appendix 19
Sapphire 234/6 numbering sequences
Extract from company memos
Sapphire 234: 'Please note the following change to instructions for numbering 4-cylinder cars:
'Car numbers
      '4230001 and onwards
'(In place of F230001 and onwards as given in DO Memo 24/1/56)'
Sapphire 234 and 236: 'Full list for numbering will now read as follows:
'Car numbers
      'Sapphire 236 6-cylinder S230001 and
         onwards
      'Sapphire 234 4-cylinder 4230001 and
         onwards
'Chassis nos
      'C230001 and onwards
'Engine nos
      'E2360001 and onwards (six cylinder)
      'E2340001 and onwards (four cylinder)
'Gearbox
      'GM230001 and onwards six cylinder
         Manumatic
      'GS230501 and onwards* four cylinder
         synchromesh'
*Added by author to complete sequence.

Appendix 20
Sapphire 234/6 overdrive serial numbers

	234	236
Overdrive unit	28/1445	28/1360*
Main casing	WN1446	WN1336
Accumulator springs	XN4968	XN4976
Thrust rings	XN1070	XN816

28/1360m when fitted with Manumatic clutch gearbox

Appendix 21
Star Sapphire engine specification
Cylinders	6
Bore	97mm/3.819in
Stroke	90mm/3.543in
Capacity	3,990cc
Compression ratio	7.5:1
Carburettor/s	
Saloon	Twin Stromberg or twin Zenith
Limousine	Single Zenith
Max power	
Saloon	165bhp at 4,250rpm
Limousine	140bhp
Max torque	
Saloon	230lb/ft at 2,000rpm
Limousine	250lb/ft at 2,000rpm

Appendix 22
Star Sapphire gearbox ratios
Saloon with Borg Warner DG automatic

Top	(direct drive)	3.77:1
Intermediate		5.41:1 to 10.82:1
Low		8.64:1 to 17.574:1
Reverse		7.574:1 to 15.148:1

Final drive ratio 3.77:1

Limousine with automatic transmission

Top	(direct drive)	4.091:1
Intermediate		5.87:1 to 12.62:1
Low		9.44:1 to 20.3:1
Reverse		8.22:1 to 17.67:1

Final drive ratio 4.091:1

Limousine with manual synchromesh gearbox

	Gearbox ratio	Overall ratio
Fourth	1:1	4.091:1
Third	1.42:1	5.81:1
Second	2.09:1	8.55:1
First	3.13:1	12.8:1
Reverse	3.31:1	13.54:1
Final drive ratio	4.091:1	

Appendix 23
Star Sapphire dimensions
Saloon
Wheelbase 9ft 6in, front track 4ft 9⅞in, rear track 4ft 9½in, width 6ft 2in, length 16ft 2in, turning circle 38ft, kerb weight approx 35½cwt.

Limousine
Wheelbase 11ft 3in, front track 4ft 10⅞in, rear track 5ft 1in, width 6ft 2½in, length 17ft 9in, turning circle 45ft, kerb weight approx 37cwt.

Appendix 24
Star Sapphire: special order colours
Factory records contain details of a number of Star Sapphires supplied to special order in paint colours other than the standard range.

Chassis number	Colour/s
33028	Special Blue
330277 and 330507	Hot Chocolate
330448	Red and Cream
330472	Red and Grey
330501	Polly Green
330522	Citrus Yellow
330642	Titanic Blue and Light Grey
330811	Metallic Red

Also finished in special colours, details not recorded, were chassis 330548, 330551, 330706, 330746, 330794 and 330819.

Appendix 25
Road test performance figures

Model	Typhoon	Whitley	Sapphire 346 Mk1	Sapphire 346 Mk1	Sapphire 346 Mk1	Sapphire 346 Mk2	Sapphire 346 Mk2	Sapphire 236	Sapphire 234	Star Sapphire
Engine	16hp	18hp	120bhp	150bhp	125bhp	125bhp	150bhp	–	–	–
Carburettors	1	1	1	2	1	1	2	1	2	2
Gearbox*	A	B	B	A	A	C	C	D	D	C
Acceleration (sec):										
0–30mph	7.6	–	4.6	4.3	–	–	–	–	–	–
0–50mph	19.5	13.5	10.1	8.9	8.5	11.4	10.0	13.2	10.9	9.3
0–60mph	29.7	19.0	15.5	13.0	12.3	16.3	14.0	18.1	15.5	12.9
Max speed (mph)	75	80	91	100	94	97	101	88	97	105
Consumption (mpg)	18-21	23-25	17-20	18.7	18-22	16.8	–	25	22-27	17
Source	Autocar	(various)	Autocar	Motor	Cars (Aus)	Autocar	Modern Motor	Modern Motor	Autocar	Autosport
Date	27/2/48	1950	17/7/53	7/10/53	2/55	20/4/55	6/55	7/57	5/10/56	26/6/59

Gearbox types: A synchromesh; B preselective; C automatic; D synchromesh with overdrive